Spelling Matters

3rd Edition

Andrew J Woods

4

Pearson Australia
(a division of Pearson Australia Group Pty Ltd)
707 Collins Street, Melbourne, Victoria 3008
PO Box 23360, Melbourne, Victoria 8012
www.pearson.com.au

First published 1993
Second edition 2002
Third edition 2008

2018 2017 2016 2015
13 12 11

Editor: Frith Luton
Text designer: Meaghan Barbuto
Typesetter: Anita Adams and Eugenio Fazio
Cover designer: Meaghan Barbuto
Cover illustration: Photolibrary Pty Ltd
Illustrations: Boris Silvestri
Printed and bound in Australia by Pegasus Media & Logistics

Pearson Australia Group Pty Ltd ABN 40 004 245 943

Acknowledgements
The publishers wish to thank the following organisations who kindly gave permission to reproduce copyright material in this book:
Phyllis Kingsbury, poem 'A spider bought a bicycle', from *A Spider Bought a Bicycle and Other Poems for Young Children*, edited by Michael Rosen, Pan Macmillan (UK), 2005: p. 71.
Robert Frost, excerpt from the poem 'Gathering Leaves', *The Poetry of Robert Frost*, Henry Holt and Co., 1923. Reprinted with permission from Henry Holt and Co.: p. 61.
Robert Frost, excerpt from the poem 'Stopping by Wood on a Snowing Evening', *The Poetry of Robert Frost*, Henry Holt and Co., 1923. Reprinted with permission from Henry Holt and Co.: p. 15.

Contents

Introduction

Welcome to *Spelling Matters Book 4.*

The *Spelling Matters* series has been developed to allow both the classroom teacher and parents to improve students' word attack skills and vocabulary range. The series provides exercises for use in the classroom and at home.

This book contains 40 work units (36 Classroom and Home Study Units and four Review Units).

The Classroom Unit

At the beginning of each unit a list of words is provided. The words in this list have a phonological, visual, morphemic or etymological relationship to each other. The Classroom Unit is a series of exercises designed to develop phonological, visual and (in the Word Building section) morphemic knowledge. Challenge words are provided at the end of each unit for vocabulary extension.

The Home Study Unit

The Home Study Unit should be completed at home, and parents are encouraged to assist their children with this unit.

The quotation, proverb or rhyme at the top of each unit shows how words from the lists have been used in our language.

The exercises in each Home Study Unit are similar in nature to those found in the Classroom Unit, although more word puzzle activities are provided.

Word Knowledge is aimed at further developing students' etymological knowledge and encourages experimentation with language.

The General Knowledge section demonstrates that the list and challenge words are not just 'spelling words', but important elements of our language. This component of each unit should provide both parent and child with a stimulating 'sharing' time. Students should be encouraged to seek help to complete this section if necessary, thereby involving parents directly in Home Study assignments. (Answers to questions in this section can be found at the end of this book.)

Provided, at the back of the book, is:

- a glossary of terms used in the units of work. Words included in the Glossary are shown in bold throughout the book.
- a Spelling Reference List containing all the List and Challenge words used in the 40 units. This list can be used by teachers, parents and students as another means of checking mastery of words.

A final note

Because language develops at different rates, students may not necessarily need to work at specified levels. Some teachers may wish to select isolated units of work related to a particular student's area of weakness.

Remember that spelling and vocabulary development should be associated with a variety of language experiences and should therefore be integrated into a total learning program.

Andrew Woods

How to use Spelling Matters

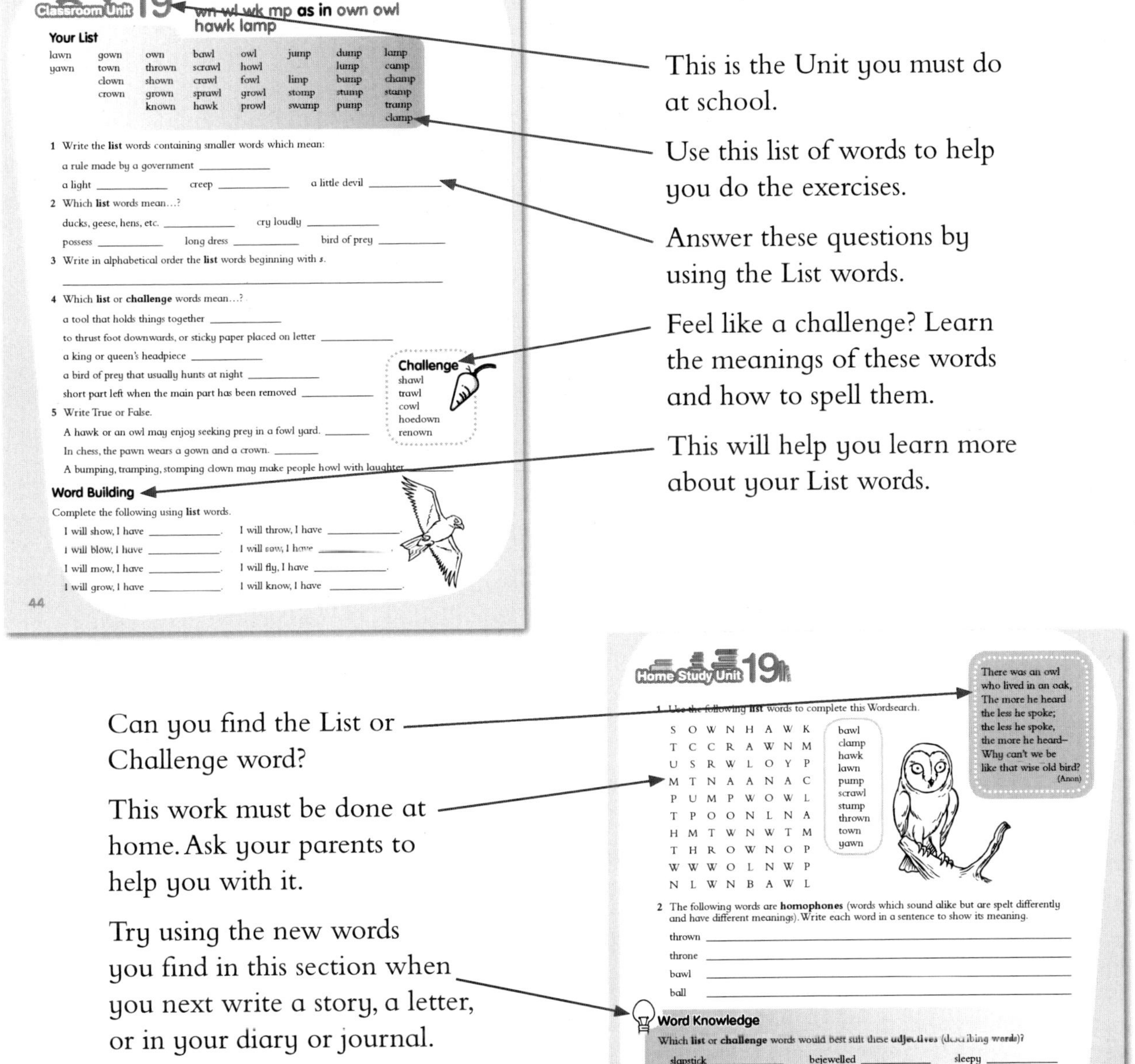

Classroom Unit 19 wn wl wk mp as in own owl hawk lamp

Your List

lawn yawn gown town clown crown own thrown shown grown known bawl scrawl crawl sprawl hawk owl howl fowl growl prowl jump limp stomp swamp dump lump bump stump pump lamp camp champ stamp tramp clamp

1 Write the **list** words containing smaller words which mean:
a rule made by a government ______
a light ______ creep ______ a little devil ______

2 Which **list** words mean...?
ducks, geese, hens, etc. ______ cry loudly ______
possess ______ long dress ______ bird of prey ______

3 Write in alphabetical order the **list** words beginning with *s*.

4 Which **list** or **challenge** words mean...?
a tool that holds things together ______
to thrust foot downwards, or sticky paper placed on letter ______
a king or queen's headpiece ______
a bird of prey that usually hunts at night ______
short part left when the main part has been removed ______

5 Write True or False.
A hawk or an owl may enjoy seeking prey in a fowl yard. ______
In chess, the pawn wears a gown and a crown. ______
A bumping, tramping, stomping clown may make people howl with laughter. ______

Challenge
shawl
trawl
cowl
hoedown
renown

Word Building
Complete the following using **list** words.
I will show, I have ______. I will throw, I have ______.
I will blow, I have ______. I will sow, I have ______.
I will mow, I have ______. I will fly, I have ______.
I will grow, I have ______. I will know, I have ______.

44

This is the Unit you must do at school.

Use this list of words to help you do the exercises.

Answer these questions by using the List words.

Feel like a challenge? Learn the meanings of these words and how to spell them.

This will help you learn more about your List words.

Home Study Unit 19

1 Use the following **list** words to complete this Wordsearch.

S	O	W	N	H	A	W	K
T	C	C	R	A	W	N	M
U	S	R	W	L	O	Y	P
M	T	N	A	A	N	A	C
P	U	M	P	W	O	W	L
T	P	O	O	N	L	N	A
H	M	T	W	N	W	T	M
T	H	R	O	W	N	O	P
W	W	W	O	L	N	W	P
N	L	W	N	B	A	W	L

bawl
clamp
hawk
lawn
pump
scrawl
stump
thrown
town
yawn

There was an owl
who lived in an oak,
The more he heard
the less he spoke;
the less he spoke,
the more he heard–
Why can't we be
like that wise old bird?
(Anon)

2 The following words are **homophones** (words which sound alike but are spelt differently and have different meanings). Write each word in a sentence to show its meaning.
thrown ______
throne ______
bawl ______
ball ______

Word Knowledge
Which **list** or **challenge** words would best suit these **adjectives** (describing words)?
slapstick ______ bejewelled ______ sleepy ______
sharp-eyed ______ bright ______ mown ______

General Knowledge
1 According to stories told by Scheherazade, how did Aladdin discover a genie?
2 At the beginning of a game of chess, which pieces number the most? ______
3 Is a hoedown something you would do ... in a car wash, ... on a dance floor or ... in a vegie garden? ______

45

Can you find the List or Challenge word?

This work must be done at home. Ask your parents to help you with it.

Try using the new words you find in this section when you next write a story, a letter, or in your diary or journal.

You may need to use reference books to help you with this section. Perhaps Mum, Dad or someone else could help.

If you are unsure of a word's meaning, look in the Glossary on page 94.
All of the words in this book can be found in the Spelling Reference List beginning on page 86. Tick the words that you can spell.
Answers are provided at the end of this book.

a _ e as in state

Your list

spade	lane	ape	daze	crate	slave
blade	mane	cape	blaze	plate	grave
trade	cane	tape	gaze	skate	shave
invade	crane	shape	maze	state	behave
	plane	scrape	graze	grate	
		grape			
		escape			

1 Which **list** words end with ***aze***? Write them in alphabetical order.

____

2 Match the following **list** words with their meanings.

lane	a fruit
crane	an animal
cape	a bird or a machine for lifting
escape	enter or attack as an enemy
grape	a thin wooden stick
ape	a narrow road
invade	a cloak
cane	get away

3 Write opposites **(antonyms)** from the **list** for:

misbehave ______________ capture ______________

Strategy

Make word sums.
For example:
m + ane = mane
sp + ade = spade.

4 Circle the correct word in the brackets in these sentences.

Tim was asked to (grate/great) the cheese before adding it to the pie.
As the iceberg moved north, a (grate/great) mass of ice fell into the sea.
The driver followed the (mane/main) highway to Sydney.
As the horse galloped down the hillside, its (mane/main) fluttered in the breeze.
We used (plane/plain) flour in the cake recipe.
The (plane/plain) taxied to the end of the runway.

Word Building

Add the ending *ing* to the following **list** words.

trade ______________ scrape ______________ blaze ______________

graze ______________ shave ______________ escape ______________

Challenge

debate	elevate	inflate	operate	vibrate	insane
humane	hurricane	amaze	barricade	lemonade	decade

> Lovely it is, when the winds are churning up the waves on the great sea, to gaze out from the land on the great efforts of someone else.
> (Lucretius)

1 Write a sentence for each of the following words.

daze ______________________________

scrape ______________________________

slave ______________________________

2 Which **list** words?

Both Batman and Superman wore one. _ _ _ _

I am a fruit used to make wine. _ _ _ _ _

You could easily get lost in me. _ _ _ _

3 An **acrostic** is a poem, or sentence, in which the first letters of each line, or word spells a word. For example: **L**ittle **A**nts **N**ever **E**at (***lane***).

Write your own **acrostic** sentence (or poem) using these **list** words.

M __________ A __________ N __________ E __________

T __________ A __________ P __________ E __________

G __________ A __________ Z __________ E __________

Word Knowledge

Which **challenge** words mean…?

ten years __________ shake __________ mad __________

drink __________ lift __________ argue __________

General Knowledge

1 What do the following have in common?

Victoria Western Australia New South Wales South Australia

____

2 What is a native of Denmark called? __________

3 Name these famous capes:

The northern-most part of Australia. Cape _ _ _ _

The southern-most tip of South America. Cape _ _ _ _

The southern-most tip of South Africa. Cape of _ _ _ _ _ _ _ _

Word History

Did you know that the word *maze* is a shortened form of *amaze*?
Can you think why?

Classroom Unit 2 are as in care

Your List

dare	care	hare	mare	fare	prepare	welfare	rare	bare	compare
spare	blare	scare	stare	glare	share	square	aware	beware	declare

1 Underline or circle the correct word in the brackets in these sentences.

The (hare/hair) escaped the fox by outrunning it.
Bettina carefully placed a (pare/pair) of scissors on the table.
Marisa brushed her (hare/hair) until the tangles had disappeared.
The old (mare/mayor) grazed peacefully in the south paddock, under the elm tree.
At the ceremony the (mare/mayor) made an emotional speech.
The rule, at Phillip's school, is that children must (ware/wear) correct school uniform.

2 Write in alphabetical order the following **list** words: ***share, scare, spare, stare*** and ***square***.

____

3 Find and write meanings for…

welfare ________________________________

declare ________________________________

Word Building

By using **prefixes** and **suffixes** these **list** words can be formed into new words.

1 fare __ __ __ __ (goodbye)

2 scare __ __ __ __ (used to frighten birds)

3 aware __ __ __ __ (having knowledge)

4 care __ __ __ (to take care)

5 care __ __ __ __ (to not take care)

6 __ __ __ __ __ mare (a bad dream)

Strategy

Look
Say
Cover
Write
Check

Challenge

ensnare
earthenware
thoroughfare
nightmare
threadbare

A trouble shared is a trouble halved.
(Proverb)

1 Which **list** word am I?

a trumpet noise ______________
an extra one ______________
not common ______________
a long fixed look ______________
divide equally ______________
to frighten ______________
strong bright light ______________
thoughtful attention ______________

2 Add ***ing*** to each of the following. Be careful!

dare ______________ care ______________ bare ______________
share ______________ spare ______________ stare ______________
glare ______________ blare ______________ prepare ______________

3 Which words, from the **list**, will fit into these Wordframes?

Word Knowledge

Which **challenge** words match these definitions?

pottery made of baked clay ______________
a public road or way through ______________
a frightening dream ______________
to trap ______________
thin and tattered ______________

General Knowledge

1 In which country is County Clare located? _ _ _ _ _ _ _

2 In Aesop's tale the _ _ _ _ was beaten in the race by the tortoise.

3 In which Australian city is Pitt Street a busy thoroughfare? _ _ _ _ _ _

Word History

In Old English a mare was an evil spirit. Therefore to dream of such things was to have a nightmare.

3 ime as in time

Your List

time	mime	lime	crime	slime	lifetime	bedtime
grime	chime	prime	overtime	playtime	meantime	sometime

1 Which of the **list** words contain smaller words that mean…?

that boy _ _ _ _ _ thin _ _ _ _ _

edge _ _ _ _ _ _ _ _ _ _ _ _ _ _ _

2 Write an interesting sentence containing: ***time, crime*** and ***grime***.

____

3 Match the meanings with the **list** words:

time for bed _ _ _ _ _ _ _

the time in between _ _ _ _ _ _ _ _

a citrus fruit or a calcium mixture _ _ _ _ first _ _ _ _ _

to ring out musically _ _ _ _ _ acting with movements _ _ _ _

4 Add ***y*** to these **list** words to form **adjectives**. The ***e*** must be dropped.

grime ______________ slime ______________

Write each of these new words in a sentence.

____

____

Word Building

Make **compound words** using the word ***time*** and the clues below.

_ _ _ _ time (extra work) _ _ _ _ time (lasting for life)

time _ _ _ _ _ _ (one who keeps time)

_ _ _ _ time (recreation period)

time _ _ _ _ _ (bus or train schedule)

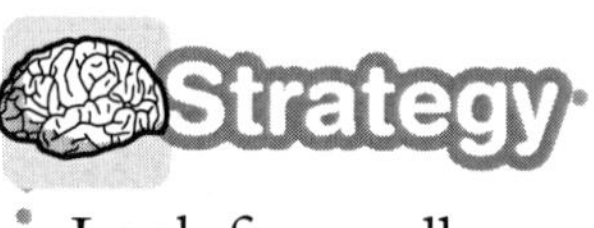

Look for smaller words.
For example:
chime = him.

Challenge

sublime
limelight
pastime
mistime
pantomime

> Lives of great men all remind us
> We can make our lives sublime,
> And, departing, leave behind us
> Footprints on the sands of time.
>
> (Henry Wadsworth Longfellow)

1 Which **list** words can you find in this Wordsearch?

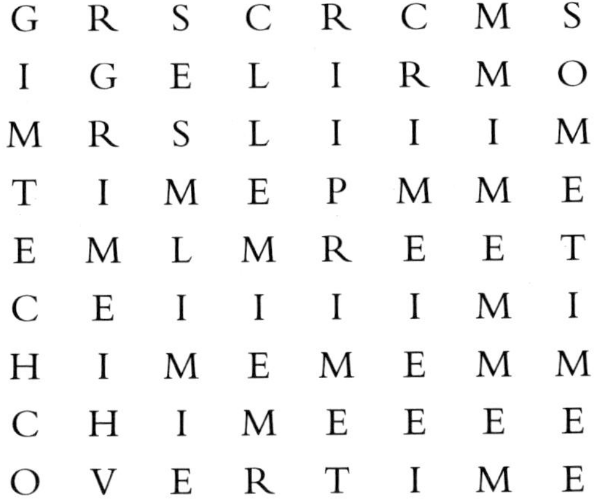

G	R	S	C	R	C	M	S
I	G	E	L	I	R	M	O
M	R	S	L	I	I	I	M
T	I	M	E	P	M	M	E
E	M	L	M	R	E	E	T
C	E	I	I	I	I	M	I
H	I	M	E	M	E	M	M
C	H	I	M	E	E	E	E
O	V	E	R	T	I	M	E

Word History

A limelight was a very bright light produced by lime in a gas flame. A limelight was used to light important actors during performances. Today the phrase 'to be in the limelight' means to have all the attention.

2 Write the most suitable **list** word in the gaps below:

As we entered the hallway, a clock was heard to _____________ softly.

The children walked from the marsh, covered with a strange green _____________.

The increasing _____________ rate was slowed down by the hard work of the police force.

Word Knowledge

Prime means of the first importance. Keeping this in mind, explain the meanings of the following:

primary school ____

prime minister ____

primitive ____

General Knowledge

1 What am I? I am an American coin worth 10 cents.
I am a _ _ _ _.

2 What sort of machine was Dr Who's Tardis? A _ _ _ _ machine

3 What am I? I am a type of play with songs usually based on a fairytale or nursery rhyme. I am a _ _ _ _ _ _ _ _ _ _.

4 ope one ome ole as in cope zone home role

Your List

role	home	zone	stone	cope	hope
dole	dome	alone	phone	lope	slope
hole	gnome	cone	throne	mope	rope
whole	chrome	tone	lone	scope	
pole		bone			

1 Write one sentence containing any three **list** words.

____

2 Use the code A = 2, B = 4, C = 6, D = 8, E = 10 etc. to find these **list** words.

8 30 26 10 __ __ __ __   8 30 24 10 __ __ __ __

38 6 30 32 10 __ __ __ __ __   2 24 30 28 10 __ __ __ __ __

3 Which **list** or **challenge** words are closest in meaning to the following words?

a meatball ____________   shiny metal ____________

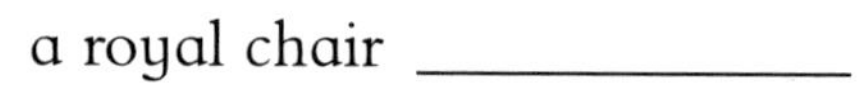

airport ____________   by yourself ____________

sulk, be in an unhappy mood ____________

a royal chair ____________   an area ____________

4 Complete these sentences using **list** words that end with ***ope***.

Peter found that he was able to ____________ with more difficult school work as he got older.

We watched as the wolf began to ____________ along the forest track.

On a rainy day there is little to do other than ____________ around miserably inside.

The answers to the quiz were well within Tina's ____________ of knowledge.

Word Building

Add ***ing*** and ***ed*** to the following **list** words. Remember the ***e*** must be dropped.

cope ____________ ____________   slope ____________ ____________

phone ____________ ____________   lope ____________ ____________

zone ____________ ____________   hope ____________ ____________

Challenge

rissole	console	aerodrome	syndrome	microscope	telephone
microphone	stethoscope	telescope	periscope	kaleidoscope	cyclone

> Home is where the heart is.
> (Proverb)

1 Write the **list** words that begin with a silent letter. ______________ ______________

2 Which **list** words best fit these illustrations?

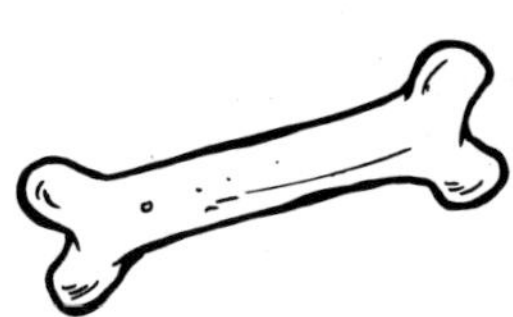

______________ ______________ ______________

3 Use the **list** words and the clues below to help you solve this Crossword.

Across
1 money paid to unemployed people
4 be in an unhappy mood
5 area

Down
1 half sphere
2 long, easy steps
3 place you live in

Word Knowledge

Which **challenge** words mean…?

a combination of things that make a certain condition _ _ _ _ _ _ _ _ _

a tropical storm with strong winds _ _ _ _ _ _ _ _

to comfort _ _ _ _ _ _ _

General Knowledge

The Latin word *scopium* and the Greek word *skopein* mean to look at or observe.

Match these ***scopes*** with what we use them for.

telescope	to look at small things
microscope	to look at to and fro movements
stethoscope	to look at things far away
periscope	to look at beautiful patterns
oscilloscope	to monitor the heart and lungs
kaleidoscope	to look around or about

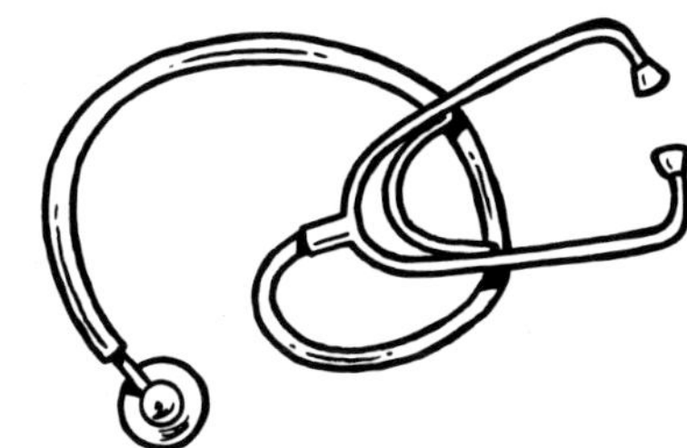

Classroom Unit 5 ee as in sheep

Your List

need, creek, greet, breed, fleet, greed, teeth, freedom, sheep, creep, bleed, knee, steep, sweep, speech, screen, speed, sleep, sweet, queen, agree, street, screech, agreed, nineteen

1 Write **list** words meaning…

to welcome ______________ a small stream ______________

to produce young ______________ to move quietly ______________

a number ______________ loud piercing noise ______________

2 Write in alphabetical order: ***sleep, speed, sheep, sweep, speech***.

____

3 Write one sentence containing any three **list** words.

____

4 Write all of the **list** or **challenge** words which contain:

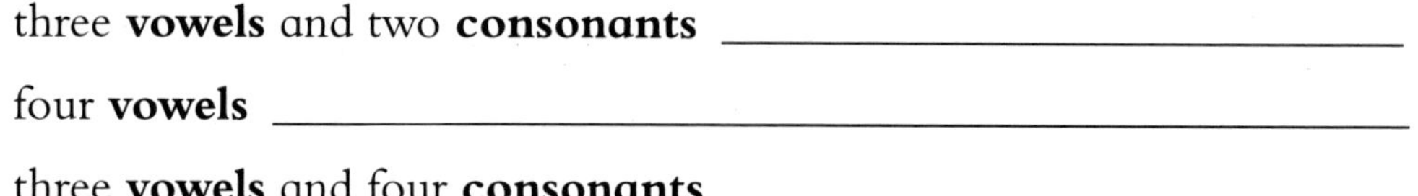

three **vowels** and two **consonants** ______________

four **vowels** ______________

three **vowels** and four **consonants** ______________

a three-letter **consonant blend** at the beginning ______________

five **vowels** ______________

5 Use a dictionary to help you write a definition, which you understand, for these words:

tweed ______________

decree ______________

discreet ______________

redeem ______________

Word Building

Can you write the **past tense** of these words? For example, agree = agreed.

breed = __ __ __ __ speed = __ __ __ __ creep = __ __ __ __ __

sleep = __ __ __ __ __ bleed = __ __ __ __ sweep = __ __ __ __ __

Challenge

proceed, discreet, tweed, guarantee, decree, esteem, degree, teepee, redeem, refugee

> The woods are lovely, dark and deep,
> But I have promises to keep,
> And miles to go before I sleep,
> And miles to go before I sleep.
> (Robert Frost)

1 Write all of the **list** and **challenge** words that rhyme with:

sheep ______ ______

______ ______

breed ______ ______ ______

______ ______ ______

greet ______ ______ ______ ______

2 Complete the following Wordsearch using nine **list** or **challenge** words. As you find the words, write them next to the Wordsearch.

S	E	E	N	C	E	T	E
W	G	R	E	E	T	E	S
E	E	S	H	E	E	T	E
E	E	C	E	R	E	C	S
P	T	R	E	S	T	S	T
H	T	E	L	L	H	H	E
S	E	E	T	E	T	U	E
E	P	C	R	E	E	K	M
E	E	H	S	P	E	E	D

______ ______

______ ______

______

______

______

______

______

3 Draw a queen with green teeth making a speech.

Word Knowledge

Which **list** or **challenge** words match the following? (A dictionary may help you!)

Native American _ _ _ _ _ _ _ a government document _ _ _ _ _ _ _

university study _ _ _ _ _ _ _ _ a suit _ _ _ _ _ _

General Knowledge

What do the following have in common?

1 Merino, Border-Leicester, Polwarth, Poll Dorset ______

2 What is the Gettysburg Address? ______

3 Where in the body is a bone called the patella? ______

6 ou as in stout

Your List

stout	trout	spout	scout	shout	sprout
cloud	proud	shroud		flour	
blouse	aloud	thousand	trousers	crouch	
drought	plough	throughout	bough	pouch	

1 Match **list** or **challenge** words with these meanings:

to call loudly _ _ _ _ _ a wicked person _ _ _ _ _ _ _ _ _

ten hundreds _ _ _ _ _ _ _ _ a tree limb _ _ _ _ _

to make the sound of _ _ _ _ _ _ _ _ _ amaze _ _ _ _ _ _ _

2 Write ***flour*** and ***flower*** in the correct places in this sentence.

The butler placed the fragrant ____________ into the vase, then went to the kitchen and carefully spooned the ____________ into the mixing bowl.

3 Write out all of the **list** words containing the smaller word ***out***.

____________ ____________ ____________ ____________

____________ ____________ ____________

4 Write in alphabetical order: ***trout, trousers, thousand*** and ***throughout***.

____

____

Strategy

Look at the shape of words. For example:

[box shape] = trout.

5 Write the **list** words containing:

two **vowels** and three **consonants** (10) ____

____

three **vowels** and three **consonants** (1) ____

Word Building

1 A city could be _ _ _ _ _ _ ed in fog.

2 How many words can you list that contain the word ***out***? For example: outback.

____

____

____

Challenge

pronoun scoundrel
flounder pronounce
astound

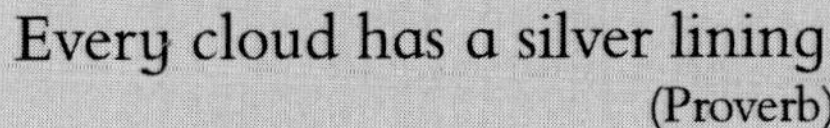

1 Replace the underlined words in these sentences with one word from either the **list** or the **challenge** words.

A cover (________________) of mist descended on the valley in the early morning.

The howling wind prevented the children from hearing Tom's loud call (________________) for help.

Little John carried a strong and heavy (________________) stick.

The grey masses of water vapour (________________) on the horizon signalled to the farmers the end of the long dry spell (________________).

2 Fill in the missing letters:

__ r __ __ s __ r s   __ __ __ __ r   __ __ o u g h

s t __ __ t   f l __ __ __ __ e r   __ r __ u d

3 A dictionary may help you to match up these meanings with the **challenge** words.

A word that stands for a **noun**, for example we, her, they, it ________________

To struggle helplessly, or a kind of fish ________________

To shock or amaze ________________

A wicked or dishonourable person ________________

4 Which **list** words could be opposites (**antonyms**) of...?

flood __ __ __ __ __ __ __ __   whisper __ __ __ __ __ __   humble __ __ __ __ __ __

Word Knowledge

Which of the **list** or **challenge** words best fit into these groups?

bud, shoot, germinate, grow ________________

yell, call, roar, exclaim ________________

villain, criminal, thief, rascal ________________

salmon, redfin, tuna, carp ________________

pocket, handbag, satchel, swag ________________

General Knowledge

1 What is Lord Baden-Powell's claim to fame? He began the __ __ __ __ __ __ movement.

2 Would a person eat, drink, climb, throw or sail a flounder? ________________

3 Which of the following is *not* a pronoun? we, her, over, it ________________

ow as in blow

Your List

bow	tow	row	sow	arrow	follow	fellow	own
blow	flow	glow	snow	narrow	hollow	yellow	bowl
grow	stow	throw	below	sparrow	borrow	bellow	
					sorrow	pillow	

1 Find words from the **list** meaning:

plant seeds _ _ _ a colour _ _ _ _ _ _ to pull along _ _ _

to have for yourself _ _ _ a line _ _ _

a knot with two loops _ _ _ a bird _ _ _ _ _ _ _

hurl or toss _ _ _ _ _ thin _ _ _ _ _ _

2 ***Bow, bowl*** and ***row*** are all **homographs**. **Homographs** are words which are spelt the same but have more than one meaning. Use the clues to write sentences to show the meaning of each **homograph**.

Bow is a piece of wood bent by string *or* a knot with two loops.

bow ______________________________

bow ______________________________

Bowl means a deep round dish *or* to throw or roll.

bowl ______________________________

bowl ______________________________

Row means to paddle *or* a line of something.

row ______________________________

row ______________________________

3 Write the following **list** words in alphabetical order:
hollow, borrow, pillow, arrow and ***follow***.

____

Strategy

Look for smaller words.
For example:
flow = low
bowl = owl.

Word Building

Add ***ing, er*** and ***ed*** to the following words to form new words.
For example row = rowing, rower, rowed.

sow ______________________________

slow ______________________________

bowl ______________________________

Challenge

tomorrow
furrow
burrow
wheelbarrow
wallow

Home Study Unit 7

> Great oaks from little acorns grow.
> (Proverb)

1 Write one sentence containing any three **list** words.

____

2 Write out all of the **list** or **challenge** words containing a smaller word which means a line of something.

____

____

3 Fill the gaps in these sentences with **list** or **challenge** words.

When watered, most plants _ _ _ _ vigorously.

The day after today is _ _ _ _ _ _ _ _.

The captain ordered all passengers _ _ _ _ _ deck during the violent storm.

On top of the mountain the _ _ _ _ was so deep that we had to _ _ _ the car to solid ground.

Spring is a time to _ _ _ vegetable seeds.

The _ _ _ _ _ whistled from Robin's _ _ _ and hit the centre of the target.

Word Knowledge

Use a dictionary to find the meanings of these words.

bellow ______________________________

wallow ______________________________

furrow ______________________________

General Knowledge

1 Name three Olympic events in which the competitors must throw an object.

____

2 What do we call today the day that is two days before tomorrow? ______________

3 Into which bay does the Yarra River flow? ______________________

Word History

The word 'tomorrow' comes from the Old English words *to morgenne*, which meant the next morning.

Classroom Unit 8

oa as in coach

Your List

roast toast coast boast float throat coach poach
groan croak cloak oath cocoa approach soak

1 Which **list** words…?

I am the sound a frog might make. _ _ _ _ _

I am a type of cape. _ _ _ _ _

I am where land and sea meet. _ _ _ _ _

I mean to get closer. _ _ _ _ _ _ _ _

I am cooked bread. _ _ _ _ _

I am a hot drink. _ _ _ _ _

2 The word ***coach*** can have at least two different meanings.
Write two sentences showing two different meanings of ***coach***.

____

____

3 Use the code A = Z, B = Y, C = X and so on to find these **list** or **challenge** words:

I L Z H G _ _ _ _ _ G S I L Z G _ _ _ _ _ _

Y L Z H G _ _ _ _ _ O L Z G S V _ _ _ _ _ _

4 How many **list** words can you make using the letters in the box?
Letters can only be used once.

f o o t c l o o t a a a t h s a t s b

______________ ______________

______________ ______________

Strategy

Make word sums.
For example:
t + oa + st
co + coa.

Word Building

Carry out these Word Equations to form new words:

coast + al = _ _ _ _ _ _ _

boast + ful = _ _ _ _ _ _ _ _

a + float = _ _ _ _ _ _

approach + able = _ _ _ _ _ _ _ _ _ _ _ _

Challenge

gloat
loathe
shoal
encroach
cockroach

Why is it with a piece of toast
(This is a fact both true and tried)
That should it land upon the floor
It's always on the buttered side.

1 Complete the Crossword using **list** words.

Across
3 a frog's call
4 cooked bread
5 promise

Down
1 brag
2 rest on top of liquid
3 where the land and sea meet

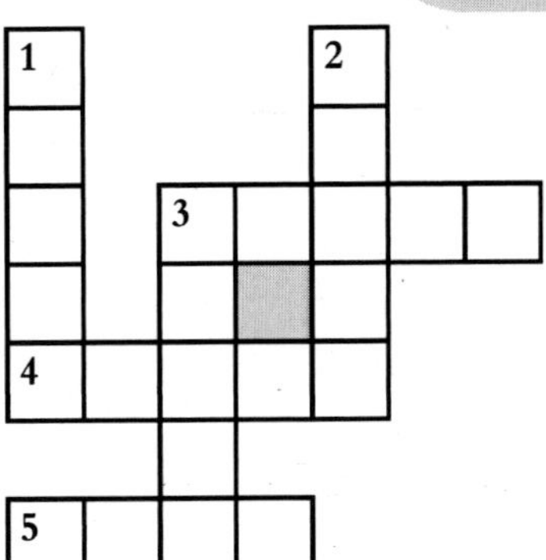

2 Which **list** word means to hunt or fish on someone's land without permission or to cook gently in liquid? ____________________

3 Write the **challenge** words that mean:

to go beyond your area _ _ _ _ _ _ _ _

a sandbank under shallow water or a group of swimming fish _ _ _ _ _

to hate _ _ _ _ _ _ _   an insect _ _ _ _ _ _ _ _ _ _ _

to gaze with evil delight or pleasure _ _ _ _ _

4 Funny Pictures. Draw a soaking coach *or* some croaking toast beside some groaning cocoa.

Word Knowledge

Add **suffixes** to complete the following.

An aid used to help someone float is called a float _ _ _ _ _ aid.

Someone you can approach with a problem is said to be approach _ _ _ _.

General Knowledge

1 Larynx, oesophagus and windpipe are all in the _ _ _ _ _ _.

2 List five major towns or cities on the east coast of Australia.

____

3 Write the name of a current Australian national coach and the sport he or she coaches. ____

ai as in fair

Your List

air	fair	hair	pair	lair	chair
stairs	fairy	repair	upstairs	dairy	flair
affair	downstairs	fairly			

Strategy

Make word sums.
For example:
f + air = fair
f + air + y = fairy.

1 Write **list** opposites (**antonyms**) for the following:

damage _ _ _ _ _ _ dark _ _ _ _

2 Which **list** or **challenge** words mean…?

two the same _ _ _ _ mend _ _ _ _ _ _

a den _ _ _ _ the gases we breathe _ _ _

3 A **homophone** is a word that sounds like another but is spelt differently and has a different meaning. Write one sentence containing the **homophones** ***stairs*** and ***stares***.

____

4 Write in alphabetical order: ***fair, chair, fairy, fairly*** and ***lair***.

____

5 Match the following with **list** words.

a lion _ _ _ _ a wand _ _ _ _ _

two socks _ _ _ _ cows _ _ _ _ _

6 Which two **list** words are **antonyms** (opposites) ______________ ______________

Word Building

How many **compound words** can you make using the following words?
For example: fair + ground = fairground. Words can be used more than once.

fair	craft	arm	ship	stairs	tight	chair	up	conditioner
ground	lift	way	tale	down	port	air	fairy	

____
____
____
____
____

Challenge

prairie
debonair
millionaire
questionnaire

… not far from Cirencester, was an apparition; being demanded whether good spirit or bad? returned no answer, but disappeared with a curious perfume and most melodious twang. Mr W. Lilly believes it was a fairy.

(John Aubrey)

1 Match the following **homophones** with their meanings.

air	a fruit
heir	two of a kind
hair	natural talent or smart style
hare	threadlike growth from the skin
pair	steps
pare	the gases we breathe
pear	looks at directly
flair	to peel
flare	one who inherits
stairs	suddenly burn brightly
stares	rabbit-like animal

2 Draw a pair of fairies sitting on a chair that needs repair.

Word Knowledge

Write **list** and **challenge** words that are **synonyms** for:

polite, cheerful, charming ______________

incident, event, occasion ______________

plain, savannah, heath, moor ______________

quite, moderately, rather, relatively ______________

Word History

The word 'pair' comes from the Latin word *par*, which means equal.
Can you think of a sport in which the term *par* is used?

General Knowledge

1 What is the name of the fairy character in the book *The Adventures of Peter Pan*?

____

2 Name two gases which make up the air that we breathe. ______________________

3 Write the title of the most famous book written by American author Laura Ingalls Wilder.

____

ea as in beam

Your List

real	seal	meal	beam	peak	neat	lean	peach
deal	steal	heal	seam	leak	heat	lead	bleach
		squeal	cream	bleak	feat	leaf	least
			stream	freak	bleat	leap	yeast
				streak	treat		leash

1 Write one interesting sentence containing any three **list** words.

____

2 Circle the correct word in these sentences.

Sometimes the moon will (seem/seam) larger when it is low in the sky.
The designer needed to sew the (seem/seam) of the trousers before finishing for the day.
The mountaineers were relieved to finally reach the (peak/peek) of Mt Snowy.
Jack could only just (peak/peek) over the wall when standing on tiptoe.
The magician performed a spectacular (feet/feat) on the stage.
Wrapped around the poor boy's (feet/feat) were rags that he had used as shoes.

3 Which **list** word am I?

I am a fruit. _ _ _ _ _

I am a sea mammal. _ _ _ _

I am a lamb's cry. _ _ _ _ _

I am the top. _ _ _ _

I am the fatty part of milk. _ _ _ _ _

I am a cord or strap for holding a dog. _ _ _ _ _

Word Building

Add the **prefix *mis*** to the following words to form new words.

lead ____________ deal ____________ treatment ____________

Add the **suffix *ly*** to the following words to form new words.

ideal ____________ real ____________ neat ____________

Add the **prefix *un*** to the following words to form new words.

leash ____________ real ____________

Challenge

conceal appeal league reveal ideal

> Look before you leap.
> (Proverb)

1 Find the **list** words, shown at right, in this Wordsearch.

V P O P E A C H I N S
L E A P I F R O E E T
B R E A L K E R F A E
A E B F R E A K E T A
Y E A S T P M H E D L
U I T M E A L D E A L

beam	peach
cream	real
deal	steal
freak	yeast
heat	meal
leap	neat

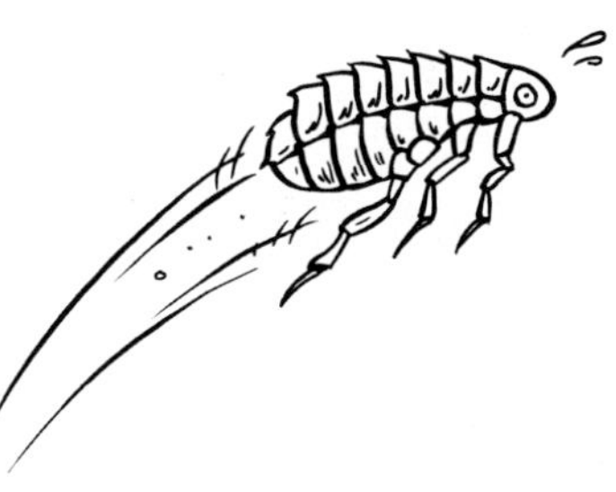

2 Find smaller words inside the **list** or **challenge** words. Use the clues to help you.

seal (the ocean) ______________ leash (remains of a fire) ______________

appeal (a green vegetable) ______________ reveal (meat from a calf) ______________

steal (a drink) ______________ least (a direction) ______________

3 Which **list** words are disguised in these shapes?

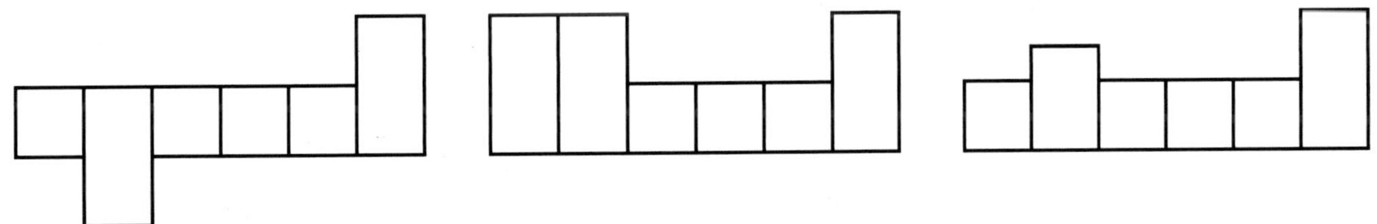

Word Knowledge

Write definitions for these **challenge** words.

conceal ____

league ____

reveal ____

ideal ____

General Knowledge

1 What ingredient makes bread rise? ______________________

2 What do the following abbreviations mean?

AFL ____

NRL ____

RSL ____

3 Who was the first to achieve the following feats?

Climb Mt Everest ______________ Step on the moon ______________

Classroom Unit 11 ea as in head

Your List

head thread breath dead ready leather spread steady feather bread tread weather instead dread meadow weapon pleasant pleasure measure treasure

1 Complete these groups using **list** words.

needle, reel, bobbin __ __ __ __ __ __

cotton, wool, fabric __ __ __ __ __ __ __

arms, legs, body __ __ __ __

pasture, field, glen __ __ __ __ __ __

2 Write all of the **list** words containing the smaller word ***read***, in alphabetical order.

____

3 Write the **list** or **challenge** words which best fit these definitions:

the state of the atmosphere ____________

to walk or step on ____________

in place of ____________

prepared ____________

4 Write **antonyms** (opposites) for:

steady ____________ dead ____________ pleasant ____________

5 Write yes or no to answer these questions.

Can you tread through a meadow? ________

Would finding treasure be dreadful or a pleasure? ________

Would a feather stay steady in windy weather? ________

Word Building

Add the following words to the **list** word ***head*** to form **compound words**.

ache quarters strong phones line land fore way

____

____

Select two of your new words and write them in one sentence.

____

____

____

Strategy

Look
Say
Cover
Write
Check

Challenge

dreadful weatherboard zealot steadfast breadth

> The thread breaks where it is weakest.
> (Proverb)

1 Which word…?

________________ ________________ ________________

2 Which **list** words best match these words?

tape ____________ ____________ chest ____________ taking

3 Write a **list** or **challenge** word in each of the following gaps.

When coming home late at night, please _ _ _ _ _ carefully through the flower garden.

It gave us great _ _ _ _ _ _ _ _ _ _ _ _ to take in the _ _ _ _ _ _ taking view.

The pirates' _ _ _ _ _ _ _ _ _ _ _ had been buried under an elm tree in the middle of the _ _ _ _ _ _.

Word Knowledge

Add *ly* to the following words to form **adverbs** (words which help to describe other words).

Change *y* to *i* before adding *ly*.	Just add *ly*.
ready ____________	dreadful ____________
steady ____________	steadfast ____________

Write the new words in the gaps in these sentences.

The suspect ____________ denied being involved in the robbery.

The experienced sailor walked ____________ across the rocking deck.

The unexpected clap of thunder frightened the children ____________.

The scouts and guides were ____________ at the service of elderly folk.

General Knowledge

1 In ancient Greek mythology Theseus killed the Minotaur in the Labyrinth of Minos.

How did Theseus find his way out of the Labyrinth? He followed a ____________.

2 Complete this saying. Slow and ____________ wins the race.

3 What am I? I am the tanned skin of an animal. ____________

Classroom Unit 12 oi as in boil

Your List

boil	soil	toil	oil	foil	coil	spoil	toilet
join	coin	point		choice	voice	rejoice	
noise	poison	moist	hoist	avoid	appoint		

1 Which **list** or **challenge** words mean…?

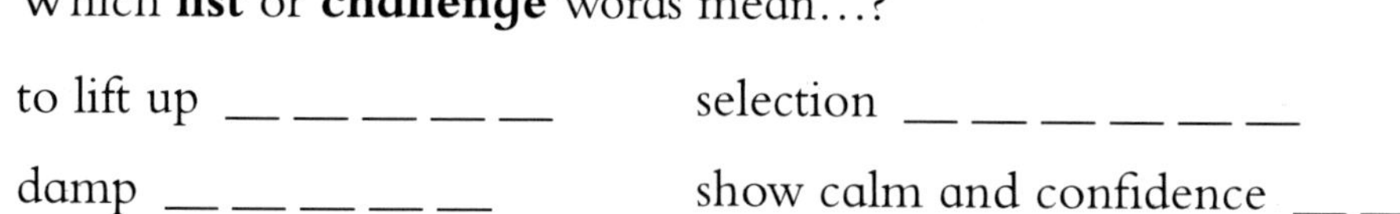

to lift up _ _ _ _ _ selection _ _ _ _ _ _

damp _ _ _ _ _ show calm and confidence _ _ _ _ _

dirt _ _ _ _ sharp end _ _ _ _ _

to work hard _ _ _ _ a rope ring _ _ _ _ _

2 Complete:

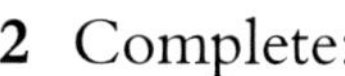

t _ _ l e t v _ _ c e p _ _ s o n a v _ _ d

3 Which **list** words contain smaller words meaning…?

a male child ________ allow ________

4 What am I?

I am a metal piece of money. ________

I am used for lubrication. ________

I mean 'to bring together'. ________

Strategy

Look at the shape of words.
For example:

= toilet

= foil.

Word Building

1 Add the endings ***ed*** and ***ing*** to the following **list** words.

boil ________ ________ toil ________ ________

oil ________ ________ foil ________ ________

coil ________ ________ join ________ ________

2 Add the **prefixes** and **suffixes** shown to make new words.

un + avoid + able = ________

moist + ure = ________

noise + less = ________

point + less = ________

appoint + ment = ________

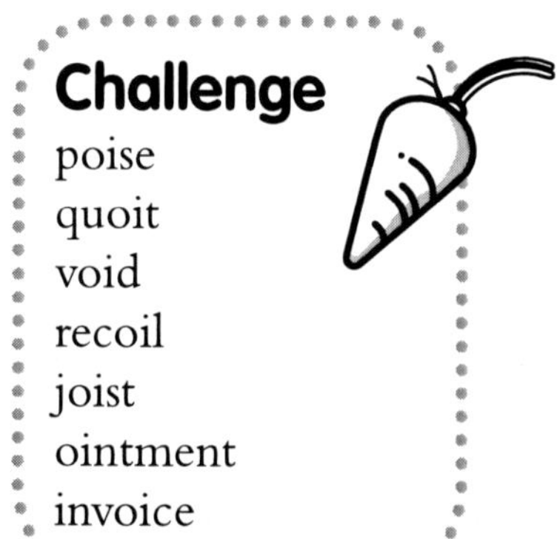

Challenge

poise
quoit
void
recoil
joist
ointment
invoice

> Double, double toil and trouble:
> Fire burn and cauldron bubble.
> (William Shakespeare)

1 Complete this Crossword using **list** or **challenge** words.

Across
1 lubricant
2 harmful liquid
5 bowl for getting rid of body waste
7 empty of everything
9 wind in loops
10 work hard
11 become hot enough to bubble

Down
1 grease to help heal
3 earth or dirt
4 sound
6 a bill or account
8 beaten metal, or light thin sword

2 Write **list** and **challenge** words which are the **antonyms** (opposites) for:

break _ _ _ _ dry _ _ _ _ _ _ laze _ _ _ _

3 Write in alphabetical order: ***point, poise, appoint*** and ***poison***.

____

Word Knowledge

Use **list** or **challenge** words to solve the following. I am a member of this family:

celebrate, make merry, be happy ______________

rapier, sabre, cutlass, claymore ______________

beam, ceiling, floorboards ______________

account, bill, receipt, voucher ______________

Word History

The word 'poison' comes from the Latin word *potio*.
Can you think of a similar word that may have come from this base?

General Knowledge

1 The famous Greek thinker Socrates killed himself by drinking hemlock.

What do you think hemlock might be? ______________

2 I am a game played with a ring. I was forbidden during the reign of Edward III of England because I was not a warlike game. ______________

3 I am a cooking method (usually for meat). I involve grilling. (I am not in the lists.)

____

ie as in tie

Your List

tie	die	lie	pie	magpie	cried
fried	flies	pied	science	society	tried

1 Write one interesting sentence containing: ***lie***, ***pie*** and ***fried***.

____

2 Which **list** or **challenge** words are disguised in these **acrostics**?

Fierce rodents invaded every desk. ____________

Some children investigated environmental needs concerning everyone. ____________

People in every town yelled. ____________

Many astonished guests poured into Expo. ____________

3 Which **list** or **challenge** word means...?

to not tell the truth ____________ bind ____________

worry ____________ having different coloured patches ____________

people living and working together as a whole ____________

study of the physical world ____________

4 Which **list** words have been formed from these words?

try ____________ cry ____________ fry ____________

5 Which **list** or **challenge** words contain smaller words that mean...?

having no hair _ _ _ _ _ _ _ untruth _ _ _ _ _

Strategy

Look
Say
Cover
Write
Check

Word Building

The **base word** for ***flies*** is ***fly***. Many words ending with ***y***, when changed to **plurals**, end with ***ies***. Change the following words to **plurals**.

spy ____________ cry ____________

butterfly ____________ sty ____________

sky ____________ fly ____________

dragonfly ____________ try ____________

Challenge

anxiety
piety
piebald

Home Study Unit 13

As a tree falls, so shall it lie.
(Proverb)

1 Write all of the **list** or **challenge** words that you can find in these pictures.

____

____

2 Use a dictionary to help you write a meaning for the word ***piety***.

____

3 Complete this Wordsearch using the following **list** or **challenge** words.

anxiety
flies
fried
society
pied
tie
lie
piety
pie

I	E	F	Y	I	P	E	F	R	L	E	F	P
P	E	I	R	E	I	I	L	F	P	I	I	E
I	A	N	X	I	E	T	Y	L	I	D	E	C
E	P	E	T	P	E	I	S	I	E	Y	P	X
D	P	I	E	T	Y	D	P	T	I	E	R	S
X	F	L	I	E	S	O	C	I	E	T	Y	I

Word History

Here is a version of how the magpie got its name.
The original name for a magpie was maggot's pie. Maggot was another name for Margaret, and Margaret's pie was a pastry with all sorts of ingredients thrown into it. The magpie in England collects all sorts of odds and ends for its nest and therefore its nest was much like Maggot's pie.

Word Knowledge

Which **list** or **challenge** words come from these words?

social ______________ anxious ______________ pious ______________

General Knowledge

1 Who am I? I am from Hamelin. I rid the town of rats but was not rewarded.

____

2 What do we call the science in which the stars and planets are studied?

____

3 What other name can also be given to the peewee or mudlark? ______________

Classroom Unit 14 ew as in dew

Your List

dew	few	new	ewe		
blew	brew	chew	crew	drew	flew
grew	knew	stew	screw	threw	
nephew	jewel	newspaper	renew	pew	

1 Which **list** words contain smaller words meaning…?

a ship or plane's work group ______________ a female sheep ______________

2 Choose **list** words to best fit the gaps in these sentences.

The son of your brother or sister is your ______________.

We watched with interest as the owl ______________ to a higher branch.

The lambs ran quickly to the side of the bleating ______________.

During the dangerous voyage the ship's ______________ abandoned the vessel after it became stranded upon a coral reef.

Children were asked not to ______________ their gum in the classroom.

3 Use the following code to find the mystery **list** words.
For example: A = B, B = C, C = D, etc.

DVD _ _ _ SGQDV _ _ _ _ _ MDOGDV _ _ _ _ _ _

4 Write meanings of the following **list** or **challenge** words.

mildew ______________________________

pew ______________________________

skewer ______________________________

shrewd ______________________________

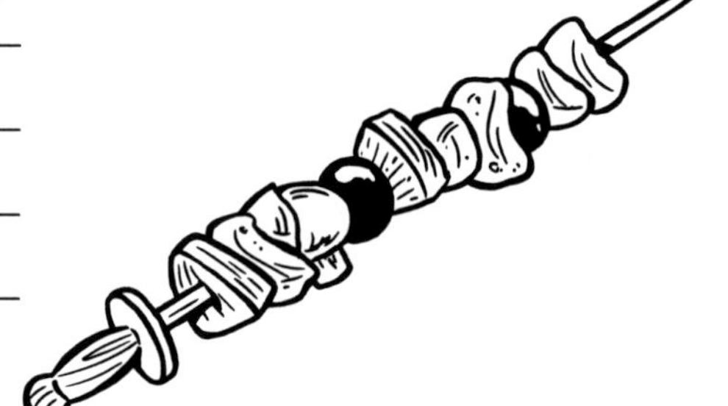

Word Building

Complete these word families.

few	few _ _	few _ _ _	blow	bl _ _	bl _ _ n
new	new _ _	new _ _ _	know	kn _ _	kn _ _ n
throw	thr _ _	thr _ _ n	grow	gr _ _	gr _ _ n

Challenge

sinew	shrewd	curlew	skewer
mildew	jewellery	curfew	shrew

Wynken, Blynken, and Nod one night,
Sailed off in a wooden shoe.
Sailed on a river of crystal light
Into a sea of dew.

(Eugene Field)

1 Which **list** words are shown here?

______ ______ ______

2 Which **list** word would fit into this Wordframe?

______

3 Which **list** or **challenge** words are **synonyms** (words with similar meanings) for the following?

gang _ _ _ _ fresh _ _ _ casserole _ _ _ _

4 Write the **list** or **challenge** words that:

begin with a **consonant** blend (for example, ***pl cr fl*** etc.) ______

______

end with a **vowel** ______

have a **consonant** blend in the middle ______

5 Which **challenge** words mean…?

a mouse-like animal ______ a seashore bird ______

a time after which people cannot be out on the streets ______

Word Knowledge

Write a match for each word. For example: mother – father.

grandmother ______ uncle ______

niece ______ sister ______

brother-in-law ______

Word History

Onomatopoeic words are words that are written the same way that they sound. For example the word 'pop' is the same as the sound it describes.

General Knowledge

1 At Midnight on December 31 you might say Happy _ _ _ Year to family and friends.

2 I am a word that is written the same as it sounds (**onomatopoeia**). I express relief, weariness, surprise etc. p _ _ _

3 I am close-fitting tartan trousers, usually worn in Scotland or Ireland. t _ _ _ _

The magic e and vowel sounds

1 Classroom Review

Your List

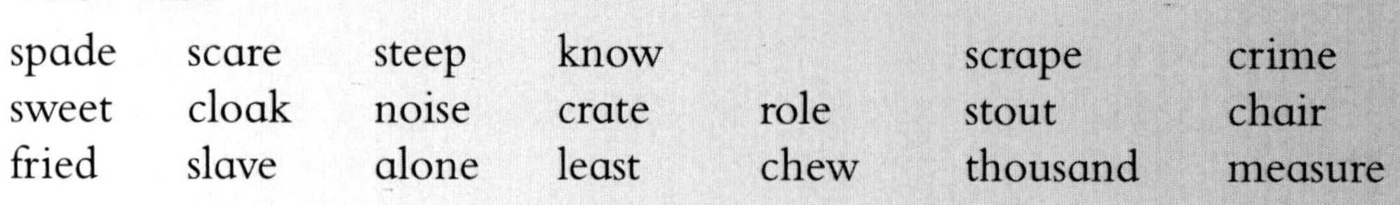

spade	scare	steep	know		scrape	crime
sweet	cloak	noise	crate	role	stout	chair
fried	slave	alone	least	chew	thousand	measure

1 Write in alphabetical order: ***cloak***, ***crate***, ***chew***, ***crime*** and ***chair***.

___

2 Write one interesting sentence containing: ***steep***, ***role*** and ***spade***.

___

3 Which **list** words mean…?

an act that breaks the law _ _ _ _ _

strong and heavy _ _ _ _ _ sugary _ _ _ _ _

smallest _ _ _ _ _ sound _ _ _ _ _

4 Use **list** words to fill the gaps in these sentences.

The children did not _ _ _ _ if they were going to the island by boat or by plane.

The recipe asked for the onions to be _ _ _ _ _ in the oil.

The actor's _ _ _ _ called for a long death scene before the final curtain.

5 Find and write the meanings of these **challenge** words.

scrumptious ___

creche ___

leprechaun ___

Look for smaller words.
For example:
crate = rat ate at
cloak = oak.

Challenge

creche leprechaun jamboree
scapegoat scrumptious

Home Study Review

> The greatest of evils and the worst of crimes is poverty.
> (George Bernard Shaw)

1 Which **list** words fit these shapes?

2 What am I?

I am ten hundreds. ______________

I am a container. ______________

You can sit on me. ______________

You can wear me. ______________

I am the opposite of most. ______________

I am an unpaid servant. ______________

3 Which **list** words are disguised in these **acrostic** sentences?

Five red inchworms entertained donkeys. ______________

Can rabbits always trick elephants? ______________

Last evening Andrew sat there. ______________

Many elegant antelopes sporting umbrellas ran everywhere. ______________

4 Which **list** words rhyme with…?

rhyme ______________ moan ______________ wait ______________

sew ______________ priest ______________ soul ______________

5 Which **challenge** words are these…?

a large gathering of scouts ______________

someone blamed for the misdeeds of others ______________

Word Knowledge

Use **list** words to fit these groups.

frighten, terrify, startle, alarm ______________

rub, scratch, rasp, graze, scour ______________

General Knowledge

1 Which of the following is not a crime?

burglary, arson, extortion, pyrotechnics, assault ______________

2 What sort of instrument would you use to measure the following?

temperature ______________ time ______________ mass ______________

3 What sort of animal is likely to 'chew the cud'? ______________

str scr spr shr thr

Your List

string	struck	scrap	spring	shrub	three	thrust
stray	straw	scrub	spray	shrug	throne	thrash
strap	stroll	scruffy	sprint	shrill	threat	through
strum	strip			shred	throb	thrill

1 Which **list** words mean…?

a special chair for royalty _ _ _ _ _ _ untidy _ _ _ _ _ _ _

a slow walk _ _ _ _ _ _ to run very fast _ _ _ _ _ _

to cut into many long thin pieces _ _ _ _ _ to push forward _ _ _ _ _ _

2 Write in alphabetical order: ***string***, ***strip***, ***scrap***, ***spray*** and ***shrug***.

____

3 Which **list** words rhyme with…?

sea __________ blue __________ pole __________

head __________ moan __________

4 Which **list** or **challenge** words contain smaller words that mean…?

to steal _ _ _ _ _ a colour _ _ _ _ _

not cooked _ _ _ _ _ small carpet _ _ _ _ _ tear _ _ _ _ _

itchy sores _ _ _ _ _ _ flat item used to carry things _ _ _ _ _

Word Building

1 Match the words in Group A with those in Group B to form **compound** words.

Group A	Group B
straw scrap	book throb
awe hair heart	berry spray struck

______________ ______________

______________ ______________

____

2 Add ***ing*** to the following words. (Remember, in these words, when adding ***ing***, the last **consonant** must be doubled.)

throb __________ scrap __________ strum __________

shred __________ strap __________ strip __________

scrub __________ shrug __________

Challenge

strict scroll shrivel thrive throttle

> I had a dove and the sweet dove died;
> and I have thought it died of grieving:
> O, what could it grieve for? Its feet were tied,
> With a silken thread of my own hand's weaving.
> (John Keats)

1 Find the **list** words that begin with ***thr*** in this Wordsearch.

T T H R E E T H R O B T
H T H R O T H R O U G H
R T H R O N E T H R E R
I R H A E T H R U S T A
L T T H R E A D H T R S
L H R T H R E A T O E H

Word History

The Greek word *thronos* means a seat above others. Which **list** or **challenge** word has come from the word *thronos*?

2 Which **list** words are shown here?

__________ __________ __________

3 Which **list** or **challenge** words contain...?

double letters ____________________

the **consonant blend *ng*** __________ __________

4 Solve these Cryptic Capers. (Clue: look for smaller words in the **list** words.)

This season ends with a ring. _ _ _ _ _ _

I am a king's single unit. _ _ _ _ _ _ _ I am a burglar's regular beat. _ _ _ _ _

I am an uncooked piece of grass. _ _ _ _ _

Word Knowledge

Which **challenge** words mean...?

choke or strangle __________ do well and become strong __________

demanding that you obey the rules __________

shrink and wrinkle __________ roll of paper __________

General Knowledge

1 What am I? I am an old fashioned word meaning three times. t h r _ _ _

2 What am I? I am an ancient country. I lie north of the Aegean Sea. I am now part of Turkey, Greece and Bulgaria. T h r _ _ _

3 Would you scrub, strum or stroll on a lute? __________

sp sk **as in** wasp mask

Your List

gasp	grasp	clasp	wasp	rasp	lisp	crisp	wisp	dusk	busk
ask	task	mask	bask	flask	risk	brisk	desk	tusk	disk

1 Complete the following sentences using **list** words.

The _ _ _ _ with the long stinging tail buzzed above the _ _ _ _ _ containing the orange juice.

Each morning, while on holidays in the Alps, we would go for a _ _ _ _ _ walk and enjoy the _ _ _ _ _ mountain air.

'If you wish to _ _ _ a question, sit at your _ _ _ _ and raise your hand,' instructed Mr Carmody.

These days you are taking a _ _ _ _ with your health if you _ _ _ _ in the sun while unprotected.

Strategy

Make words sums.
For example:
m + ask = mask
gr + asp = grasp.

2 Which **list** words mean…?

to grip tightly _ _ _ _ _ a face covering _ _ _ _

something small, thin and delicate _ _ _ _ scrape or rub roughly _ _ _ _

a job to do _ _ _ _ not being able to pronounce 's' _ _ _ _

3 Answer Yes or No.

Does a wasp fly with a lisp? ____________ Is a task kept in a flask? ____________

Is it dangerous to grasp a moving tusk? ____________

Word Building

1 Add *ed* and *ing* to the following **list** words.

gasp	________	________	clasp	________	________
lisp	________	________	bask	________	________
risk	________	________	grasp	________	________
ask	________	________	rasp	________	________

2 Select any two of your new words and write one interesting sentence containing both.

____

____

Challenge
kiosk
will-o'-the-wisp
casket
obelisk

Home Study Unit 16

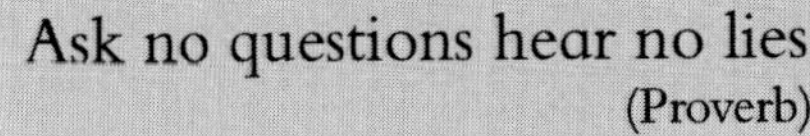

Ask no questions hear no lies.
(Proverb)

1 Which **list** words would fit in these Wordframes?

2 Which **challenge** words mean…?

a stone column ______________ a small jewellery box or coffin ______________

3 An **acrostic** poem is one in which the first letter of each line spells a word.
Try writing an **acrostic** poem yourself, using any of the **list** words.

Moths ______________

Are battering themselves ______________

Suicidally like ______________

Kamikaze pilots. ______________

4 Which **list** words are shown here?

______________ ______________

Word History

Kiosk is a Turkish word that means pavilion. Although originally a 'dancing' flame of light seen over marshy ground, *will-o'-the-wisp* has come to mean someone who is elusive or not easily caught.

Word Knowledge

By adding ***y*** to some of the **list** words they become **adjectives** (describing words).
Add ***y*** to the words below.

wisp ______________ crisp ______________ risk ______________

Now match the new words to the **nouns** they describe.

carrots ______________ rescue ______________ clouds ______________

General Knowledge

1 What sort of snake did Cleopatra, Queen of Egypt, use to kill herself? _ _ _

2 What am I? I am a coarse file with separate teeth. _ _ _ _

3 What do the following have in common? Paper European Mud ______________

Classroom Unit 17 rt rd rm rn rk rf rp rb

Your List

dart	port	card	farm	corn	ark	surf
part	sort	hard	harm	horn	bark	scarf
chart	fort	bird	warm	born	dark	harp
heart	short	word	storm	worn	mark	sharp
	hurt	herd	worm	turn	shark	herb
	skirt	forward		burn	work	
	shirt	towards		return	cork	

Look at the shape of words. For example:

bird hard herd hurt dart fort bark dark herb.

1 Which **list** words mean…?

a bottle stopper __ __ __ __ plant used for medicine or cooking __ __ __ __

a flying animal __ __ __ __ the body's blood-pump __ __ __ __ __

savage fish __ __ __ __ __ to come back __ __ __ __ __ __

2 Choose **list** words to write in the gaps in these sentences.

One of the first tasks for the day on Auntie Sal's __ __ __ __ is to feed the chooks and geese.

Captain Clark checked his __ __ __ __ __ to find out where the dangerous reefs were located.

Your birthday is the day when you celebrate the day you were __ __ __ __.

3 Which three **list** words are items of clothing?

__________ __________ __________

4 Which **list** words beginning with ***w*** rhyme with…?

term __________ jerk __________ form __________

5 Which **list** or **challenge** words are **antonyms** (opposites) for…?

backward __________ light __________ blunt __________ soft __________

6 What am I?

I am a musical instrument. __________ I am a ship's home. __________

Word Building

Add **list** or **challenge** words to the following to make **compound words**.

__________ board __________ board __________ fish

__________ wood __________ house __________ stile

__________ night __________ hand __________ ache

Challenge

guard uniform dwarf superb sword squirm warp disturb

> The Sun's rim dips; the stars rush out:At one stride comes the dark.
> (S.T. Coleridge)

1 Draw a surfing shark wearing a warm scarf.

2 Which **list** words are **synonyms** (words with similar meanings) for these…?

type ______________ portion ______________ rotate ______________

brief ______________ scorch ______________ scratch ______________

3 Find three **list** words containing a smaller word that is a body part. Write them here.

______________ ______________ ______________

Word Knowledge

1 Complete the following 'card' words.

(stiff paper) card __ __ __ __ __ (throw away) __ __ __ card

(a large notice or poster) __ __ __ card (to do with the heart) card __ __ __

(a knitted woollen jacket) card __ __ __ __

2 Which **challenge** words mean…?

to wriggle about ______________ twist out of shape ______________

a weapon ______________ magnificent ______________

General Knowledge

1 This is a place where you can go to play

____

2 What am I? I am a major river in north Western Australia. I flow into the Joseph Bonaparte Gulf. ______________________________

3 On what might you find the following? lanyard, epaulettes, badges of rank

____

18 lt ld lk lf lb lm lp

Your List

salt	volt	cold	bald	myself	elf	bulb
halt	bolt	gold	wild	yourself	calf	calm
felt	silk	fold	world	himself	half	palm
belt	milk	sold	should	herself	wolf	
melt	talk	hold	could	itself	gulf	gulp
adult	difficult	build	would		golf	help

1 Which **list** words mean…?

a magical creature ______________ an onion-like root ______________

a measurement of electric force ______________ a sport ______________

swallow quickly ______________ a large bay ______________

2 Write in the missing letters to make **list** words.

s __ __ t h __ __ f p __ __ m t __ __ k

3 Write three different questions beginning with: ***should***, ***would*** and ***could***.

____?

____?

____?

4 Which **list** words are **synonyms** (words with similar meanings) for these…?

crease __ __ __ __ stop __ __ __ __ Earth __ __ __ __ __ hairless __ __ __ __

5 Which **list** words belong in these groups…?

fig, oak, wattle, eucalypt ______________ kitten, puppy, lamb, foal ______________

cheese, cream, butter ______________ ice, freeze, snow, shiver ______________

Word Building

1 A **contraction** is a shortened word that has been made from two words. Write the following **contractions** in full.

shouldn't ______________ couldn't ______________ wouldn't ______________

2 To change most words ending with ***lf*** to plurals, change the ***f*** to ***v*** and then add ***es***. Make the following **list** words into **plurals**.

elf ______________ calf ______________ half ______________ wolf ______________

Challenge

baulk hulk mould engulf whelp

All the world's a stage
And all the men and
women merely players.
(William Shakespeare)

1 Use **list** words to complete this Crossword.

Across
1 precious metal
4 touched
5 wild dog
6 construct
7 hairless

Down
2 hard
3 a little fairy
4 crease
6 onion-like root

2 Which **list** words...?

______ ______ ______ ______

3 Write True or False.

Gold is one of the world's most precious metals. ______

Mould grows on a bald head. ______

Salt melts on a cold morning. ______

Word History

The Latin word *adultus* means grow up. Which **list** word comes from this base? 'Adolescent' also comes from the same base. Use a dictionary to help you write a meaning for adolescent.

Word Knowledge

1 Write an interesting sentence containing: ***baulk*** and ***hulk.*** ______

______

2 Write meanings for:

whelp ______

engulf ______

mould ______

General Knowledge

1 Which war began as a result of a search for WMDs in 2003? _ _ _ _ War

2 Which villain is common to these characters? Three Pigs, Peter, Red Riding Hood

______

3 What name is given to an adult female fox? ______

wn wl wk mp as in own owl hawk lamp

Your List

lawn	gown	own	bawl	owl	jump	dump	lamp
yawn	town	thrown	scrawl	howl		lump	camp
	clown	shown	crawl	fowl	limp	bump	champ
	crown	grown	sprawl	growl	stomp	stump	stamp
		known	hawk	prowl	swamp	pump	tramp
							clamp

1 Write the **list** words containing smaller words which mean:

a rule made by a government ______________

a light ______________ creep ______________ a little devil ______________

2 Which **list** words mean…?

ducks, geese, hens, etc. ______________ cry loudly ______________

possess ______________ long dress ______________ bird of prey ______________

3 Write in alphabetical order the **list** words beginning with *s*.

____

4 Which **list** or **challenge** words mean…?

a tool that holds things together ______________

to thrust foot downwards, or sticky paper placed on letter ______________

a king or queen's headpiece ______________

a bird of prey that usually hunts at night ______________

short part left when the main part has been removed ______________

5 Write True or False.

A hawk or an owl may enjoy seeking prey in a fowl yard. ________

In chess, the pawn wears a gown and a crown. ________

A bumping, tramping, stomping clown may make people howl with laughter. ________

Challenge

shawl
trawl
cowl
hoedown
renown

Word Building

Complete the following using **list** words.

I will show, I have ______________. I will throw, I have ______________.

I will blow, I have ______________. I will sow, I have ______________.

I will mow, I have ______________. I will fly, I have ______________.

I will grow, I have ______________. I will know, I have ______________.

There was an owl
who lived in an oak,
The more he heard
the less he spoke;
the less he spoke,
the more he heard–
Why can't we be
like that wise old bird?
(Anon)

1 Use the following **list** words to complete this Wordsearch.

S	O	W	N	H	A	W	K
T	C	C	R	A	W	N	M
U	S	R	W	L	O	Y	P
M	T	N	A	A	N	A	C
P	U	M	P	W	O	W	L
T	P	O	O	N	L	N	A
H	M	T	W	N	W	T	M
T	H	R	O	W	N	O	P
W	W	W	O	L	N	W	P
N	L	W	N	B	A	W	L

bawl
clamp
hawk
lawn
pump
scrawl
stump
thrown
town
yawn

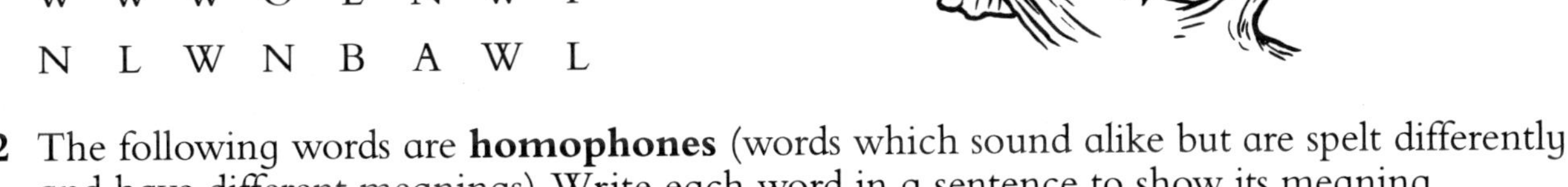

2 The following words are **homophones** (words which sound alike but are spelt differently and have different meanings). Write each word in a sentence to show its meaning.

thrown ______________________________

throne ______________________________

bawl ______________________________

ball ______________________________

Word Knowledge

Which **list** or **challenge** words would best suit these **adjectives** (describing words)?

slapstick ____________ bejewelled ____________ sleepy ____________

sharp-eyed ____________ bright ____________ mown ____________

General Knowledge

1 According to stories told by Scheherazade, how did Aladdin discover a genie?

____

2 At the beginning of a game of chess, which pieces number the most? ____________

3 Is a hoedown something you would do … in a car wash, … on a dance floor or … in a vegie garden? ____________

20 nch as in bench

Your List

winch	inch	flinch	pinch	bench	clench	trench	stench
drench	ranch	branch	hunch	crunch	lunch	punch	

1 Write in alphabetical order: ***clench***, ***crunch***, ***branch***, ***hunch*** and ***bench***.

____

2 Use a dictionary to help you find the meanings of the following words.

winch ______________________________

flinch ______________________________

hunch ______________________________

drench ______________________________

wrench ______________________________

quench ______________________________

3 Which **list** words mean…?

nip or squeeze sharply ____________ close or press tightly ____________

midday meal ____________ hit with clenched fist ____________

strong unpleasant smell ____________

4 Write an interesting sentence containing any three **list** words.

____

5 Which **list** words contain smaller words meaning…?

the number after nine ____________ breakfast cereal ____________

a sharpened piece of metal used as a fastener ____________

Word Building

To make words ending with ***ch*** plural, just add ***es***. Change the following words to **plurals**.

winch ____________ bench ____________ branch ____________

ranch ____________ lunch ____________ punch ____________

trench ____________ pinch ____________ hunch ____________

Challenge

quench wrench

> Dirty water will quench fire.
> (Proverb)

1 Select any five **list** words. Use each word in five different sentences.

____

____

____

____

____

2 Which **list** words fit the following Wordframes?

3 Which **list** words mean…?

a device for hauling and hoisting ______________

to bend or arch into a hump ______________

to move a very short distance at a time ______________

to soak or make very wet ______________

Word History

The word 'ranch' comes from the Spanish word *rancho*, meaning a group of people who eat together.

Word Knowledge

Quench is a **homograph**—a word spelt and sounding the same as another, but with a different meaning. Write two sentences, each containing the word ***quench*** used in different ways.

____

____

General Knowledge

Match the branch of science with what it studies.

Branch of science	**Study of**
Anthropology	civilisation through material remains
Biology	birds
Astronomy	animals
Geology	living organisms
Archaeology	humankind
Sociology	heavenly bodies
Ornithology	earth
Zoology	society

dge nge rge nce **as in** edge range large once

Your List

edge	hedge	ledge	judge	ridge	bridge	dodge	badge	distance
barge	large	charge		gorge				advance
hinge	fringe	range	strange	change	plunge	orange		entrance
chance	dance	glance		since	prince		once	balance

1 Which **list** words mean…?

a way built over a river, roadway or railway ______________

a narrow shelf ______________ a narrow valley with steep walls ______________

a flat-bottomed boat ______________ odd ______________ son of a king ______________

2 Fill the gaps in these sentences with suitable **list** words.

Many fairytales begin with the words, '______________ upon a time'.

At the end of the trial the ______________ sentenced the burglar to five years' jail.

'I wish you'd cut your __________,' said the mother to her son for the umpteenth time.

3 Which **list** or **challenge** words would best fit into these groups?

waltz, tango, ballet ______________ court, lawyer, magistrate ______________

mountains, hills, plateau ______________ lemon, lime, mango ______________

valley, gully, canyon ______________ duke, baron, earl ______________

4 Write two different meanings for ***gorge***.

____

Word Building

Add ***ing*** to the following words. Remember to drop the final ***e*** before adding the ending.

charge ________________ glance ________________ plunge ________________

dodge ________________ dance ________________

barge ________________ advance ________________

exchange ________________ balance ________________

Use memory triggers.
For example:
edge of the ledge
c (see) one once.

Challenge

knowledge urge
exchange trudge
sponge

> Will you, won't you, will you, won't you will you join the dance?
>
> (Lewis Carroll)

1 The following **list** words are written in a code based upon this pattern.

so edge =

What are these words?

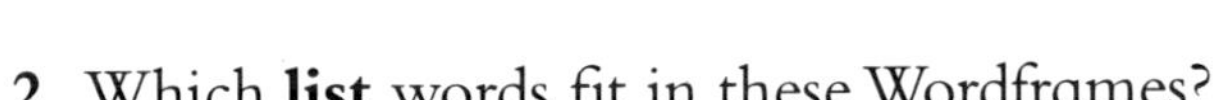

2 Which **list** words fit in these Wordframes?

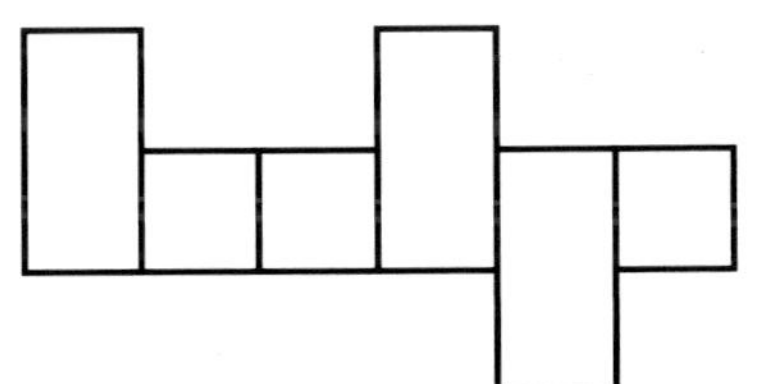

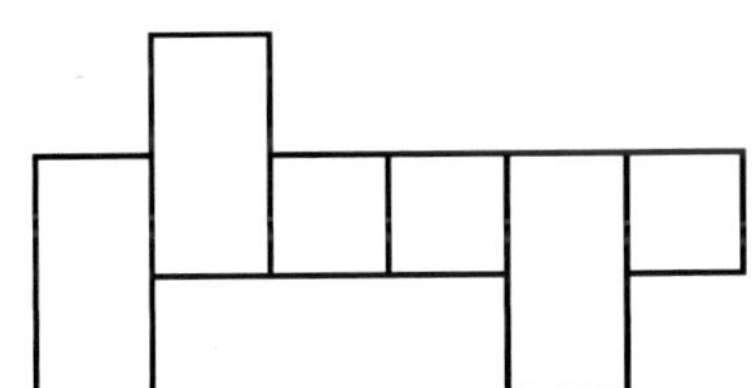

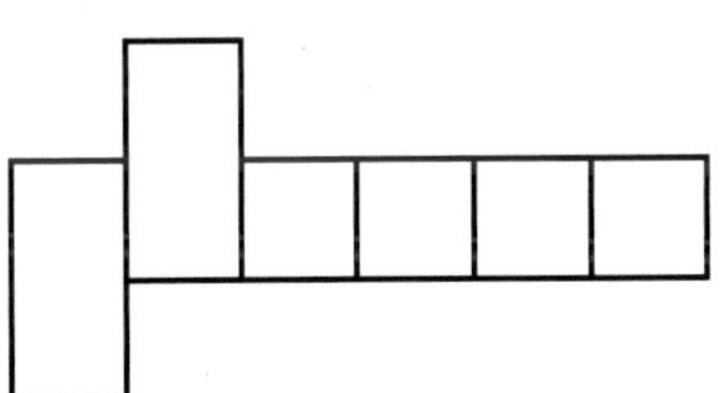

Word Knowledge

Match these definitions with the **list** or **challenge** words:

go forward ______________________

a light cake ______________________

to push or drive forwards ______________

to make things equal ______________

far away place ______________________

way in ______________________

walk wearily ______________________

trade ______________________

information known ______________

a fruit or colour ______________

General Knowledge

1 What do we call a beaver's home? ______________________

2 In which cities are these famous bridges?
Harbour Bridge, Tower Bridge, Golden Gate Bridge

____

3 In which Australian states are these gorges?

Geikie Gorge ______________ Katherine Gorge ______________

Jasper Gorge ______________ Wittenoom Gorge ______________

Word History

The word 'prince' comes from a Latin word *princeps*, which means chief or leader.
Can you think of a word, from the same base, for the chief or leader at your school?

22 ght as in thought

Your List

bought fought ought sought thought brought nought
caught taught naughty draught fortnight

1 Fill the gaps in these sentences with **list** words.

We used a roll of cloth to block the ______________ blowing in under the door.

At the supermarket we ______________ a week's supply of groceries.

The paintings had been ______________ from Europe for the display in the gallery.

The children had been ______________ to cross the busy road safely.

The batter made his way back to the dressing room after being ______________ out by a fielder.

2 True or False? ***Caught***, ***taught*** and ***draught*** rhyme with ***fort***. ______________

3 Which **list** words are the **antonyms** (opposites) for…?

took ___________ dropped ___________ learnt ___________ sold ___________

Word Building

Write the **list** words matching the following:

buy ______________ bring ______________ think ______________
fight ______________ catch ______________ teach ______________

Write a sentence containing at least two of these words.

____

____

Think about the shape of words. For example: all of the list words end with this shape.

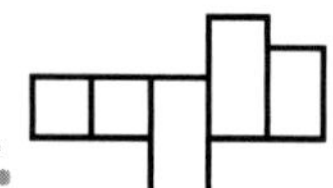

Challenge

wrought fraught distraught

Home Study Unit 22

Thought is free.
(William Shakespeare)

1 Which **list** words would fit in these Wordframes?

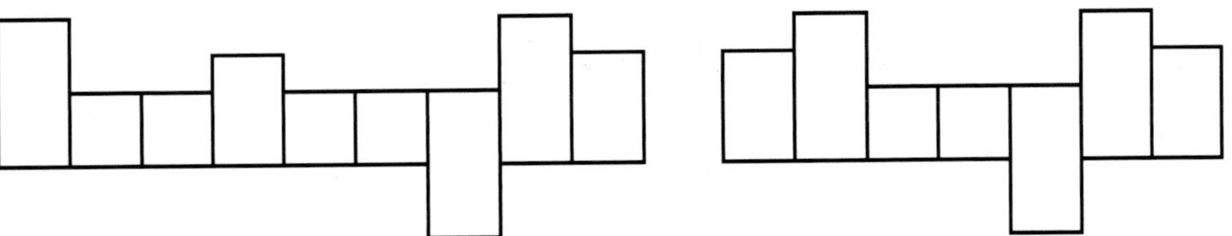

2 Which **list** words mean…?

having had a fight __________

two weeks __________

bound to __________

nothing __________

gave knowledge __________

looked for __________

current of air or wind __________

3 The words ***bought*** and ***brought*** are often confused. ***Bought*** means having used money to buy something. ***Brought*** means having been able to bring something.
Write each word in a sentence.

____

____

4 Which three **list** words do not rhyme with ***court***?

__________ __________

____

Word History

Did you know that the word *fortnight* comes from the words *fourteen nights*?

Word Knowledge

Match these definitions with **challenge** words.

full of (as in: The move was __________ with danger.) __________

shaped by beating with a hammer (as in: __________ iron) __________

General Knowledge

Name any two countries that fought on the Allied side in the following wars:

World War One __________ __________

World War Two __________ __________

The Gulf War 2003 __________ __________

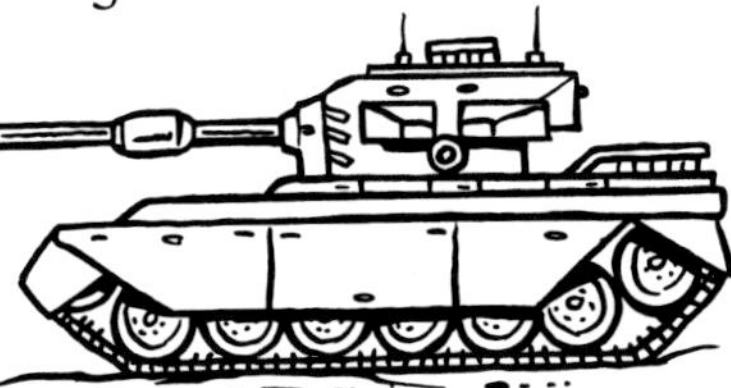

Consonant beginnings and endings

Your List

strong	scratch	sprint	shrill	throat	grasp	dusk	squirt	forge
lord	reward	warn	fern	spark	turf	sport	firm	
tilt	vault	child	shelf	known	thump	munch	brought	

Classroom Review 2

1 Write an interesting sentence containing: ***strong***, ***brought*** and ***vault***.

____

2 Which **list** words mean...?

tip to one side _ _ _ _ a young person _ _ _ _ _

hard _ _ _ _ a clump of earth _ _ _ _ a plant _ _ _ _

evening _ _ _ _ an underground room _ _ _ _ _

to move forward with great effort _ _ _ _ _ _

3 Write in alphabetical order: ***spark***, ***strong***, ***shelf***, ***squirt*** and ***scratch***.

____

Strategy

Look
Say
Cover
Write
Check

4 Find some smaller words contained in the following **list** words.
Example: sport = port

sprint = ____________ grasp = ____________

known = ____________ spark = ____________

5 Write all of the **list** words that would be found between ***strap*** and ***turtle*** in a dictionary.

____

6 Which **list** words rhyme with...?

vote ____________ colt ____________ worm ____________

Word Building

Words written in the **past tense** are words which show that something has already happened. Change these words to make them **past tense**. For example: reward = rewarded.

scratch ____________ sprint ____________ know ____________

bring ____________ thump ____________ squirt ____________

tilt ____________ forge ____________ vault ____________

Challenge

surge arrange
musk wizard

> Child! do not throw this book about;
> Refrain from the unholy pleasure
> Of cutting all the pictures out!
> Preserve it as your chiefest treasure.
>
> (Hilaire Belloc)

1 Find all the **list** and **challenge** words beginning with ***s*** in this Wordsearch.

R E P S H E L F A S
P S P I R L I T U C
W A T K I B T S S R
S Q Y R S R I Q P A
U T H J O S P U A T
R S I P H N S I R C
G F S P I H G R K H
E V S P R I N T D C

2 An **acrostic** sentence or poem is one in which the first letter of each word or line spells a word. On a separate piece of paper, use a **list** or **challenge** word to write your own **acrostic**.

Example: **L**ittle **o**tters **r**an **d**aintily *or*

Lights flashing, brilliant **c**olours
Opals in the sky
Rocketing into the
Darkness

3 Which **list** words fit into these Wordframes?

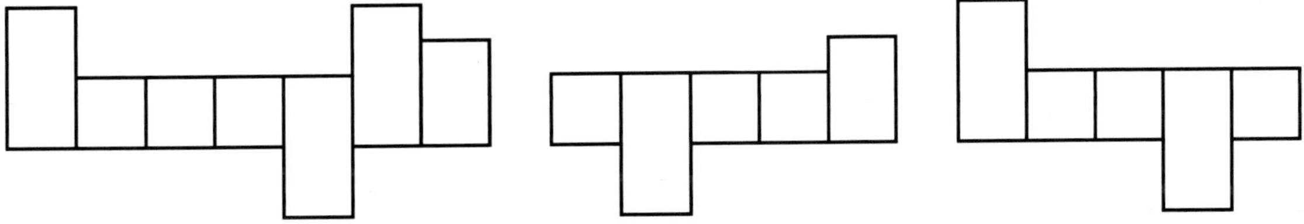

Word Knowledge

1 Which **challenge** words would best match the following?

a magical wand ______________ a perfume ______________

2 What might a tidal surge be? ____

General Knowledge

1 Name any three sports in which a ball must be struck with a bat.

____

2 What is the main language spoken in France? ______________

3 What is the name of the lost girl in *The Wizard of Oz*? ______________

Word History

The word *wizard* comes from the words *wise person*.

Classroom Review 2

Classroom Unit 23

Plurals: s ss sh ch x

Your List

atlas	mess	flash	touch	hatch	tax
circus	hiss	clash	pouch	match	
	toss	splash	branch	watch	
	guess	brush	church		
	dress	bush			

1 Re-write all the **list** words, making them all **plural**, in the box above.

2 Which **list plurals** mean…?

books of maps ______________

the sounds snakes make ______________

upward throws ______________ timepieces ______________

places where people gather to worship ______________

Strategy

When **nouns** end in ***s***, ***ss***, ***sh***, ***ch*** or ***x***, add ***es*** to form the plural.

3 Choose a **list plural** to write in the gaps in these sentences.

All that could be heard were the ______________ of lapping water against the jetty poles.

The clown had performed in ______________ all of his life.

In the distance the ______________ of lightning grew brighter as the ______________ of thunder became louder.

Kangaroos carry their joeys in their ______________.

Word Building

Complete the following. The first one is done for you.

splash	splashed	splashes	splashing
branch	______________	______________	______________
clash	______________	______________	______________
guess	______________	______________	______________
toss	______________	______________	______________
match	______________	______________	______________

Challenge

addresses sandwiches platypuses radishes fortresses

Saw the firefly, Wah-wah-taysee,
Flitting through the dusk of evening,
With the twinkle of its candle
Lighting up the brakes and bushes.
(Henry Wadsworth Longfellow)

1 Write the plurals of the words ***clash***, ***watch***, ***brush***, ***bush***, ***tax*** and ***atlas*** in alphabetical order.

____

2 Which **list** plurals?

____________ ____________ ____________

3 Which **list** or **challenge plurals** match the following?

portholes, galleys, cabins, gangways ____________

mosques, temples, synagogues ____________

sundials, eggtimers, clocks ____________

Ashton's, Barnum & Bailey, Moscow ____________

carrots, potatoes, cabbages ____________

leaves, trunks, roots ____________

4 Draw platypuses in dresses eating sandwiches.

Word History

When the first platypus was seen by Europeans they could not believe what they were seeing. The word 'platypus' comes from the Greek word *platupous*, which means flat-footed.

Word Knowledge

1 Which **challenge** words are **synonyms** (words with similar meanings) for the following?

castles ____________ residences ____________

2 Which **challenge** words mean…?

Australian monotremes ____________ defences ____________

sliced bread with fillings ____________ salad vegetables ____________

General Knowledge

1 What are we? We are round juicy fruits with furry skins. We are related to apricots and nectarines. ____________

2 What are we? We are large flightless birds from Africa. When frightened we are supposed to bury our heads in sand. ____________

3 What sort of characters open the play *Macbeth* by Shakespeare? ____________

Plurals: y as in jury

Your List

jury dairy diary
hobby trophy ferry
family factory century
daisy country company

RULE: For **nouns** that end in a **consonant** and ***y***, form the **plural** by dropping ***y*** and adding ***ies***. For example: cherry becomes cherr***ies***.

1 Re-write the words in the **list**, making them all **plural**, in the box above.

2 Which **list plurals** mean…?

passenger boats ______ pastimes ______ nations ______

flowers ______ records of daily events ______

buildings where goods are made ______

3 Choose a **list plural** to write in the gaps in these sentences.

The children had been asked to keep ______, in which they wrote every day.

Many ______ have passed since the fall of the Roman Empire.

France, Italy and Spain are all European ______.

Word Building

1 Write the names of these berries in full. For example: straw + berries = strawberries.

rasp ______ black ______ blue ______

goose ______ boysen ______ cran ______

2 Complete:

one hobby, many ______

one company, two ______

one ceremony, several ______

one daisy, a field of ______

one library, many ______

one country, a group of ______

one memory, many ______

one trophy, a shelf full of ______

Challenge

memories libraries strawberries ceremonies

Strategy

Change the ***y*** to ***i*** and add ***es***.

Buttercups and daisies,
Oh, the pretty flowers:
Coming 'ere the Springtime,
To tell of sunny hours.
(Mary Howitt)

1 Which **list plurals** or **challenge plurals** match the following?

______ ______ ______ ______

2 Write in alphabetical order: ***diaries***, ***daisies*** and ***dairies***.

______

3 Use the clues and **list** and **challenge plurals** to solve this Crossword.

Across
1 places for storing milk
4 passenger boats
7 places from which books can be borrowed
8 daily records

Down
1 flowers
2 awards
3 places of manufacture
4 parents and children
5 fruits
6 pastimes

Word Knowledge

Which **list plurals** best fit into the following groups?

judges, magistrates, barristers, solicitors ______

medallions, ribbons, prizes ______

stamps, coins, models ______

hydrofoils, tankers, tugboats ______

roses, daffodils, gladioli ______

General Knowledge

1 What are we? We are related to kangaroos although smaller. w_ _ _ _ _ _ _ _

2 What is the name given to places where plants are raised and sold? n_ _ _ _ _ _ _ _

3 What is the name of the books in which the meaning of words can be found? d_ _ _ _ _ _ _ _ _ _ _

Word History

Before the invention of paper, the thin inner bark of certain trees was used for writing on. In Latin this bark was called *liber*.

Which **challenge** word might come from *liber*?

25 Plurals: vowel followed by y

Your List

spray	relay	turkey	alley	______
donkey	monkey	valley	holiday	______
birthday	journey	delay	highway	______

______

RULE: For **nouns** ending in ***y*** following a **vowel**, form the **plural** by adding ***s***. For example: valley becomes valley***s***.

Strategy
Vowel before *y*:
add *s* to make plural.

1 Re-write the words in the **list** box, making them all **plural**.

2 Write in alphabetical order:
sprays, ***turkeys***, ***valleys***, ***donkeys*** and ***alleys***.

______

3 Change the following words to **plurals** and then write an interesting sentence containing each one.

holiday ______

delay ______

4 Which **list plurals** mean…?

team races ______ vacations ______ apes ______

5 Write **list** or **challenge plurals** in the gaps in these sentences.

The children celebrated their ______ together on Saturday.

The tourists had travelled on many ______ during their trip around Australia.

The blaze was brought under control after many powerful ______ from the firefighting helicopter.

After several ______ the cricket match eventually got under way.

Word Building

Join words in Group A to those in Group B to form new **compound words**.

Group A		**Group B**			
high	sea	ways	days	______	______
alley	birth	sprays	ways	______	______

Challenge
buoys galleys

Home Study Unit 25

> The monkeys say:
> 'Come on, let us play,'
> And they frisk in the
> coconut trees.
> (Eugene Field)

1 Write **list** and **challenge plurals** in rhyming groups.

Rhyming with ***trees*** Rhyming with ***trays*** Rhyming with ***toys***

____

____

____

2 What are we?

We are passageways between buildings. ______________

We are hold-ups or stoppages. ______________

We are the days upon which we celebrate our birth. ______________

3 Draw turkeys, donkeys and monkeys enjoying their holidays.

Word History

Did you know that once the only holidays were on Holy Days?

Word Knowledge

1 Use a dictionary to help you find the meanings of the following words.

galleys ______________ *or* ______________

buoys ______________

2 Which **challenge** and **list** words best fit in these groups of words?

roads, freeways, byways ______________

kitchens, cookhouses, bakeries ______________

markers, floats, capstans ______________

voyages, travels, tours ______________

General Knowledge

1 What was the name given to the low carts, without sides, used for hauling logs, wool bales and other heavy loads through the bush? d _ _ _ _

2 What is the name given to underground passages, built especially for pedestrians and trains? s _ _ _ _ _ _

3 Write the names of three valleys in the state where you live.

____

Classroom Unit **26**

Plurals: f/fe to ves

Your List

half	leaf	calf
thief	wolf	life
loaf	knife	self
shelf	wife	elf

Strategy

Some words ending in *f* or *fe* change *f*/*fe* to *v* then add *es*.

RULE: For some **nouns** ending with ***f*** or ***fe***, you form the **plural** by changing the ***f*** or ***fe*** to ***v***, and then adding ***es***. For example: el**f** becomes el**ves**.

1 Re-write the words in the **list** box as **plurals**.

2 Which **list plurals** mean…?

supports for books or ornaments ______________ robbers ______________

young cows ______________ dog-like mammals ______________

bread ______________ small fairy beings ______________

fractions meaning one of two equal parts ______________

3 Write one sentence containing the **plurals** of ***leaf***, ***life*** and ***wife***.

____

4 Write the **plurals** of ***loaf***, ***life***, ***shelf***, ***wife*** and ***wolf*** in alphabetical order.

____

Word Building

The **plural** of ***self*** is often used with the words ***them***, ***our*** and ***your*** to form ***themselves***, ***ourselves*** and ***yourselves***. Use these words to fill the gaps in these sentences.

'I am busy working so you must look after ______________,' called Mother.

The children had hidden ______________ under the hay.

'We shall make sure that we have made ______________ comfortable before we bed down for the night,' explained the leader of the bushwalkers.

Challenge

sheaves yourselves ourselves themselves

Spades take up leaves
No better than spoons,
And bags full of leaves
Are as light as balloons.
(Robert Frost)

1 Find all of the **list plurals** in this Wordsearch.
(Note: One word will be found in other words.)

L	E	A	V	E	S	S	E	S	S	L	H	V	T
I	H	V	S	W	E	S	H	E	L	V	E	S	H
V	A	L	E	W	E	L	V	V	O	A	A	S	I
V	L	A	V	V	A	I	L	I	A	E	L	E	E
E	V	C	L	C	L	W	O	L	V	E	S	V	V
S	E	E	L	V	K	N	I	V	E	S	L	I	E
C	S	A	C	A	L	V	E	S	S	C	A	W	S

2 Draw autumn leaves *or* thieves running for their lives *or* loaves on shelves.

Word Knowledge

Although the following words end in ***f***, to make them **plural** we just add ***s***.
For example: roof becomes roof***s***.

gulf ____________ dwarf ____________ staff ____________ chief ____________

Hoof, ***scarf*** and ***wharf***, when changed to **plural**, can be written with either ***ves*** or ***s***.

General Knowledge

1 What is the name given to bundles of corn, wheat and so on, tied together and left standing in fields? s _ _ _ _ _ _

2 How many wives did Henry the Eighth have? ____________________

3 What sort of creatures would you be watching at the zoo if you were watching lupines loping about? ____________________

Plurals: change of basic spelling

Your List

foot ______	mouse ______	woman ______
goose ______	man ______	tooth ______
ox ______	child ______	louse ______

RULE: For some words there is a change in the basic spelling to form **plurals**.

1 Match the following **plurals** with **list** words, and write them in your **list** box.

children mice oxen women teeth
feet geese lice men

2 Which four **list plurals** have different Wordframes from their singular form?

______ ______ ______ ______

3 Which **list plurals** mean…?

small wingless insects that live in the skin or hair _ _ _ _

bone-like growths in the mouth used for chewing _ _ _ _ _

small rodents _ _ _ _ web-footed farmyard birds _ _ _ _ _

bullocks _ _ _ _

4 Write an interesting sentence containing any three **list plurals**.

______

Word Building

Complete:

one ox, several ______

a child, a group of ______

a woman, many ______

one goose, a gaggle of ______

one foot, a pair of ______

a man, many ______

Challenge
gentlemen
crises

Look at the shape of words. For example: tooth, teeth.

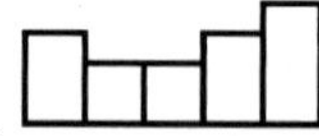

Home Study Unit 27

The children were nestled all snug in their beds,
While visions of sugar-plums danced in their heads.
(Clement C. Moore)

1 Write these **list plurals** in alphabetical order: ***men***, ***mice***, ***oxen***, ***feet***, ***teeth*** and ***children***.

____

2 Which **list plurals**...?

__ o __ __ n   __ e __ __ e   __ e __ __ h

3 Match **list plurals** with these illustrations.

__________   __________   __________

4 Write the singular of ***crises*** and then use a dictionary to help you write a definition.

__________ ______________________________

Word Knowledge

Which **list** words are best related to the following?

ganders __________   drays and wagons __________

moccasins and gumboots __________   molars and incisors __________

General Knowledge

1 How many feet would you expect to find on...?

an insect __________   a spider __________

a bird __________   a snake __________

2 What do nits usually grow into? __________

3 What do the following have in common?

incisors, molars, wisdom, canine __________

Classroom Review 3

Plurals

Your List

marsh	berry	display	child	______
bunch	reply	jockey	fox	______
baby	knife	torch	story	______
thief	class	cherry	mouse	______

1 Re-write the words in the **list** box, making them **plural**.

2 Change the following sentences so that the **nouns** are **plurals**. For example: 'The fox walked through the marsh', becomes, 'The fox*es* walked through the marsh*es*'.

The child used his torch to find his way.

______

It is dangerous to leave a sharp knife near a baby.

______

The display showed a bunch of cherries.

______

3 Write an interesting sentence containing the **plurals** of: ***story***, ***child***, ***thief***.

______

4 Which **list plurals** mean…?

boggy places ______ horse riders ______ answers ______

tales ______ shows ______ cutting tools ______

Word Building

Make **compound words** by joining words from both groups.
Then write the new words as **plurals**.

straw	book
fairy	field
carving	

knife	berry
story	shelf
mouse	

New word	Plural
______	______
______	______
______	______
______	______
______	______

Challenge

varnishes
boundaries
mysteries
wretches
decoys
bookshelves

Learn the rules for making plurals.

A cat in gloves catches no mice.
(Proverb)

Classroom Review 3

1 All but one of the sixteen **list plurals** are hidden in this Wordsearch. Which is the missing word?

J D I S P L A Y S B A B I E S
O C S E S I E S A B S U T C C
C C L A S S E S S E A N H H L
K L S T H N E V I E S C E I T
Y A T M O U S R H S R H V L H
S I O C H E R C E L E E S D I
M A R S H E S H I D N S E R E
I E I I B S C M O U S E S E V
C S E E S R E P L I E S I N E
E E S J O C K E Y S F O X E S
A I E T S I C H E R R I E S S

The missing word is: ______________

2 Which **list plural** would best fit into this Wordframe?

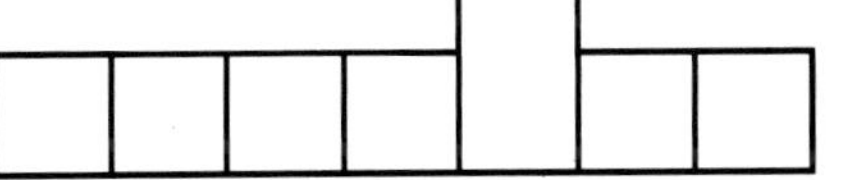

3 Complete the following.

a mouse, a nest of ______________

a display, a room full of ______________

one thief, a den of ______________

one cherry, a bunch of ______________

a child, a class of ______________

a berry, a bowl of ______________

4 Write one sentence containing any three **list plurals**.

____

Word Knowledge

Which **plurals** of **challenge** words mean…?

baffling puzzles ______________

limits ______________

unfortunates ______________

baits or lures ______________

book ledges ______________

hard glossy coats ______________

General Knowledge

1 What name is given to the people who ride horses in competitive races? ______________

2 What types of stories are Cinderella, Goldilocks, and Hansel and Gretel? ______________

3 What do the following have in common? Mickey, Mighty, Danger, Town and Country?

____

Classroom Unit 28

Homonyms—Homophones

Your List

piece peace
brake break
which witch
their there they're
cell sell
threw through
night knight
blue blew
wear where
metre meter
to too two
wood would
right write
our hour

1 Circle the correct word in brackets in these sentences.

After the thief (threw/through) his loot (threw/through) the open window, he climbed (threw/through) it himself.

My teacher asked me if I could (right/write) with my left hand as well as with my (right/write).

All of the students placed (their/there) packs over (their/there) where (their/there) leader had pointed.

We had arrived at (our/hour) destination one (our/hour) earlier than expected.

The (would/wood) cutter (would/wood) take his load of firewood to market each Friday.

Dorothy had a great deal of trouble deciding (which/witch) (which/witch) was a good (which/witch).

If you do not step on the (brake/break) soon enough, you may (brake/break) either the machine or yourself.

After many years of fighting over a barren (piece/peace) of land, the countries decided to make (piece/peace) with each other.

(Where/wear) winds blow bitterly it is wise to (where/wear) warm clothes.

2 Which **list** words best fit these clues?

In days gone by I wore a suit of armour. ______________ I follow day. ______________

I am one hundred centimetres. ______________ I am a measuring instrument. ______________

Word Building

Add the **suffix** or **prefix** shown to make new words from these **list** and **challenge** words.

peace + (ful) ______________
break + (fast) ______________
knight + (hood) ______________
night + (fall) ______________
meter + (box) ______________
(over) + seas ______________
(kilo) + metre ______________
(fire) + wood ______________
right + (ful) ______________
(centi) + metre ______________
where + (abouts) ______________
seize + (ure) ______________

Challenge

current currant check cheque seas seize

It takes two to speak the truth–
one to speak and another to hear.
(Henry Thoreau)

1 Write an interesting sentence containing: ***blue***, ***blew***.

____

2 Which **list** words rhyme with the following?

site ________ ________ ________ ________

stitch ________ ________

true ________ ________ ________ ________ ________ ________ ________

3 Write definitions for *cell* **and** *sell.*

____

4 Write an interesting sentence containing: ***night***, ***knight***.

____

5 Draw a witch choosing which broomstick to use *or* a knight's nightwear.

Word Knowledge

Write a suitable **list** or **challenge** word for each of these groups.

raisin, sultana, dried fruit ________

accelerator, battery, clutch, gears ________

kilogram, minute, litre, decibel ________ *or* ________

indigo, cobalt, sapphire, azure ________

gauge, clock, compass ________

jail, prison, cage, dungeon ________

grab, capture, grip, clasp ________

General Knowledge

1 Complete the following.
100 centi________ = 1 ________ 1000 ________ = 1 kilometre

2 What do the following have in common?
Yellow, Red, Black, Caspian, Caribbean ________

3 What sort of person do we address as 'Sir'? ________

29 Compound Words

Your List

airport	clockwork	background	silkworm	basketball	cupboard
overnight	rainforest	headline	daylight	everything	afternoon
pullover	stagecoach	headlight	shoplift	lifeboat	lighthouse

1 These **compound words** have been mixed up. Can you unscramble them to find ten **list** words?

basketnight clockworm ______ ______

overhouse everycoach ______ ______

cupball silkwork ______ ______

lightnoon afterlight ______ ______

stageboard headthing ______ ______

2 Write an interesting sentence containing: ***lifeboat*** and ***lighthouse***.

______

3 Which **list** words mean…?

working like a clock ______ a jumper to pull over the head ______

boat for saving lives ______ the time after midday ______

all things ______ a forest that receives heavy rainfall ______

the main light ______ the light of day ______

4 Fill the gaps in these sentences with suitable **list** words.

The artist had painted strangely shaped trees in the ______ of his painting.

The cargo ship was headed for certain disaster before the captain spotted the beacon at the top of the ______.

Because it was getting late Martha and Terry decided to stay ______ at Grandma's.

Strategy

Make word sums.
For example:
shop + lift
life + boat.

Word Building

1 Add ***board*** to the following words to form new words.

cup ______ spring ______ surf ______

chalk ______ over ______

2 Add ***light*** to the following words to form new words.

day ______ head ______ ______ house

______ weight ______ year

Challenge

briefcase
tongue-tied
extraordinary

> Everything comes to those who wait.
> (Proverb)

1 Which **list** words would fit in these Wordframes?

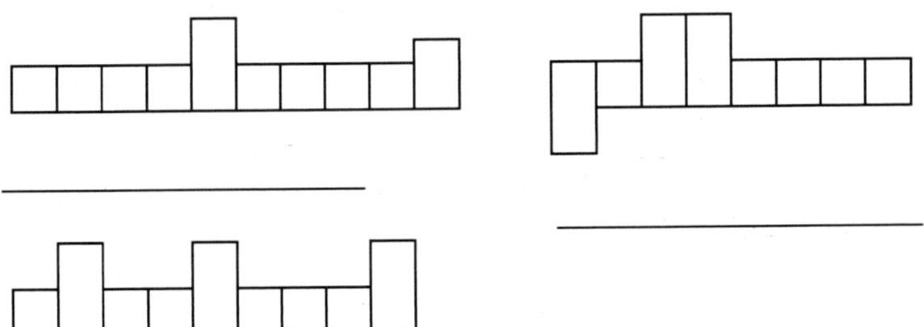

Word History

Dr James Naismith invented a game in 1892 in which players tried to score by throwing a ball into peach baskets.
Which sport do you think Naismith invented?

2 Use the code A = 1, B = 2, C = 3 etc. to help you find these disguised **list** words.

12 9 6 5 2 15 1 20 ______________ 19 20 1 7 5 3 15 1 3 8 ______________

2 1 3 11 7 18 15 21 14 4 ______________ 1 6 20 5 18 14 15 15 14 ______________

3 Write in alphabetical order: ***basketball***, ***background***, ***briefcase***, ***airport*** and ***afternoon***.

____

Word Knowledge

Which **list** or **challenge** words best fit into these groups?

grasslands, desert, mountains, plains, woodland ______________

backpack, suitcase, handbag ______________

cardigan, sweater, windcheater, jerkin ______________

softball, baseball, football, volleyball ______________

remarkable, unusual, wonderful ______________

harbour, station, helipad ______________

stammering, stuttering, umming and ahing ______________

General Knowledge

1 Which **list** word might you think of when you see these company names?

Virgin Blue, Qantas, Singapore ______________

Omega, Seiko, Swatch ______________

2 With which sport do you associate the following?
Boomers, Kings, Tigers, Capitals, Bulls, Lakers, Opals, Titans ______________

3 In which Australian state is the Daintree rainforest? ______________

Prefixes: super under sub bi

Your List

supermarket superstar
underarm underground underline underwear
subway submarine subzero undergrowth
subtitle submerge bicycle biceps

Split the word into **prefix** and the rest of the word. For example: super/star.

1 The **prefix** ***super*** can mean of a higher quality, or going beyond. Which **list** or **challenge** word means...?

high quality shopping place ________________ going faster than sound ______________

going beyond the natural world _____________ going beyond stardom ______________

2 The **prefix** ***under*** means below. Which **list** or **challenge** words mean...?

below the ground ________________ a line below ________________

shrubs or small trees growing below large ones ________________

clothes worn under outer clothes ________________ below the arm ________________

3 The **prefix** ***sub*** means lower position, under, or second in importance. Which **list** or **challenge** words mean...?

passageway under the road _____________ secondary title _____________

under the sea _____________ to go under _____________

lower than zero _____________

4 The **prefix** ***bi*** means two. Write a definition for ***bicycle***.

____

5 How many muscles make up the biceps? _____________

6 Choose any three **list** words and write them in an interesting sentence.

____

Word Building

Add the **prefix** ***under*** to the following words to form new words.

________ developed ________ carriage ________ clothes ________ hand

________ tow ________ world ________ water ________ pass

Challenge

supersonic supernatural undercarriage bilingual
superficial superstition subscription

A spider bought a bicycle
And had it painted black
He started off along the road
with an earwig on his back
He sent the pedals round so fast
he travelled all the day
Then he took the earwig off
And put the bike away.
(Phyllis Kingsbury)

1 Solve these picture puzzles to find **list** or **challenge** words.

____________ ____________ ____________

2 Which **list** words:

might you wear? ________________ might you shop in? ________________

might you use your legs to ride? ________________

might be a way to bowl a ball? ________________

might you travel underwater in? ________________

3 Which **list** words contain smaller words meaning…?

circular _ _ _ _ _ _ _ _ _ _ _ _ us _ _ _ _ _ _ _ _ _ _

a stain, spot or scratch _ _ _ _ _ _ _ _ _ _ _ _

thick, black sticky substance _ _ _ _ _ _ _ _ _ _

Word Knowledge

Replace the underlined words in these sentences with **list** or **challenge** words, which are **synonyms** (words with the same meaning) for them.

The children explored the <u>subterranean</u> (________________) caves.

The pedestrians walked through the <u>tunnel</u> (____________) to the other side of the road.

On the hill stood an old house that was said to be haunted by <u>unearthly</u> (________________) spirits.

The captain ordered his <u>submersible machine</u> (________________) to submerge to a depth of 40 metres.

General Knowledge

1 In which part of your body would you find your biceps? ____________

2 What are boneshakers, velocipedes and tandems? ____________

3 Does water freeze at subzero temperatures? ____________

Classroom Unit 31 Suffixes: ing

Your List

_______________ _______________ _______________ _______________ _______________

_______________ _______________ _______________ _______________ _______________

_______________ _______________ _______________ _______________ _______________

_______________ _______________ _______________ _______________ _______________

_______________ _______________

1 Add the **suffix *ing*** to the following words and then write the new words in the **list** box above. (These are your **list** words for Classroom and Home Study Unit 31.)

stop	shop	begin	skip	swim	whip	spin	plan	trot	split
flap	slip	plot	step	stir	prod	chop	grip	run	throb
snap	swap								

2 Which **list** words are **synonyms** (words with similar meanings) for the following?

poking _______________ pacing _______________ grasping _______________

halting _______________ lashing _______________ preparing _______________

exchanging _______________ starting _______________ revolving _______________

3 Use **list** words to complete the following sentences.

Through the glass bottom of the boat we could see hundreds of fish _______________ in and out of the coral reef.

The criminals had been _______________ the robbery for many months.

Dread filled the hearts of the sailors when they realised that the flag which was _______________ on the mast of the approaching ship was the Jolly Roger.

The woodcutters spent the day firstly _______________ then _______________ the wood and finally stacking it behind the shed.

Word Building

Complete the table:

Base word	Add *ed*	Add *ing*
shop	shopped	shopping
whip	_______________	whipping
skip	_______________	skipping
flap	_______________	_______________
step	_______________	_______________
grip	_______________	_______________
throb	_______________	_______________
snap	_______________	_______________

Strategy

Where there is a vowel followed by a consonant, you double the final consonant before adding *ing*.

Challenge

starring
spanning
sparring
worshipping

> When the first baby laughed for the first time,
> the laugh broke into a thousand pieces
> and they all went skipping about and that
> was the beginning of fairies.
> (J.M. Barrie)

1 Write a **list** word to best describe the following. For example: a ***swimming*** fish

a ____________ flag a ____________ headache

a ____________ top a ____________ crocodile

2 Write the **list** words that begin with ***p*** in alphabetical order.

____

3 Write an interesting sentence containing any two **list** or **challenge** words.

____

4 Draw a slipping runner and a running slipper.

5 Which **list** words would fit in this Wordframe?

____________ ____________ ____________

____________ ____________ ____________ ____________ ____________

Word Knowledge

Which **challenge** words mean…?

featuring the main actors ____________ reaching across ____________

showing great honour, love and respect ____________ boxing ____________

General Knowledge

1 In which Olympic sport did Ian Thorpe and Jodie Henry make their names? ____________

2 What sorts of events are the following?

marathon, 100 metres, Stawell Gift, Otway Classic ____________

3 In Australia, what was the sport of harness racing originally called? ____________

Classroom Unit 32 Contractions

Your List

couldn't	wouldn't	shouldn't	that's	where's	they've	you've	doesn't
hadn't	don't	can't	isn't	didn't	who's		won't

1 Write the **list** words that match the following.

where is ______________
who is ______________
that is ______________
is not ______________
does not ______________
should not ______________
do not ______________
they have ______________
did not ______________
will not ______________
you have ______________
would not ______________
can not ______________
had not ______________

2 Write an interesting sentence containing ***can't*** and ***don't***.

____

3 Write a question for each of the following **list** words.

Can't ____?

Didn't ____?

Where's ____?

Doesn't ____?

Wouldn't ____?

Word Building

Re-write the following sentences, changing the underlined words to **contractions**.

The searchers <u>could not</u> look for the lost children until first light.

____

'<u>Do not</u> run across the road!' screamed the teacher.

____

'<u>That is</u> the way we should go,' explained the scout leader.

____

'No, you <u>can not</u> go out to play,' insisted Mum.

____

Challenge

aren't should've could've

An **apostrophe** shows that one or more letters are missing.

Those who live in glass houses shouldn't throw stones.
(Proverb)

1 Write one sentence containing any two **list** words.

____

____

2 Write these **contractions** in full.

where's ________	they've ________	didn't ________
can't ________	shouldn't ________	don't ________
that's ________	isn't ________	won't ________

3 Write in alphabetical order: ***that's***, ***they've***, ***don't***, ***didn't***, ***doesn't***.

____

4 Which **list** words would fit in these Wordframes?

Word Knowledge

Write each of the **challenge** words in interesting sentences.

____

____

____

General Knowledge

Write five safety rules (school, road, home, water etc.) beginning with the word ***don't***.

Don't ____

Don't ____

Don't ____

Don't ____

Don't ____

Classroom Unit 33 Homonyms—Homographs

Your List

file	post	rear	cross	spell	cape	punch	chest
mind	hide	seal	loaf	match	mole	stick	train

1 Which **list** words mean…?

an animal skin *or* keep from being seen ______________

say the letters of a word *or* a magic chant ______________

angry *or* two lines passing through each other ______________

a fruit drink *or* hit with a clenched fist ______________

a wooden firelighter *or* someone/something equalling something else ______________

the back of something *or* to raise a child *or* stand on back legs ______________

front part of your upper body *or* strong box with hinged lid ______________

mail *or* job or duty *or* upright piece of wood ______________

cloak *or* land jutting into the sea ______________

orderly collection of papers *or* a steel tool ______________

a sea mammal *or* to close tightly ______________

laze about *or* an amount of bread ______________

part of you that thinks and feels *or* to look after ______________

a furry underground animal *or* a dark skinspot ______________

railway carriages joined together and pulled along *or* to teach a person or animal to do something ______________

long thin piece of wood *or* to glue or fasten ______________

2 Which **list** words…?

s __ __ __ l   __ __ __ d   m __ t __ __   __ r __ __ s

Challenge

pound
staple
vault

Word Building

1 Add ***ing*** (careful!)

file + ing = ____________   hide + ing = ____________   staple + ing = ____________

2 Change the following words to **plural**.

match ____________   loaf ____________   cross ____________   punch ____________

3 Add the words in brackets to form **compound words**.

post (card) ____________   spell (bound) ____________   (tea) chest ____________

match (stick) ____________   (meat) loaf ____________

Home Study Unit 33

A crooked stick will have a crooked shadow.
(Unknown)

Keep true, never be ashamed of doing right; decide on what you think is right and stick to it!
(George Eliot)

1 Which **list** words are shown here?

______________ ______________

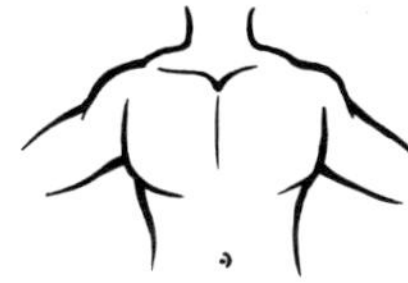

______________ ______________

2 Write the following **homographs** in sentences showing both their meanings.
For example: The <u>cross</u> teacher drew a large red <u>cross</u> on Robert's work.

post ______________

chest ______________

match ______________

Word Knowledge

Which **list** or **challenge** words best fit into these groups?

walrus, whale, dugong, dolphin ______________

left hook, uppercut, jab ______________

bay, peninsula, isthmus, point ______________

locomotive, engine, carriage, diesel ______________

jump, leap, bound ______________

General Knowledge

1 Name two Olympic events that require an athlete to vault. ______________

2 Where might a bank keep its valuables? ______________

3 Where might a lost dog be kept? ______________

4 Which note of currency is used in England? ______________

Compound Words

Your List

blackout	overhead	seahorse	fairground	evergreen	cardboard
everybody	spotlight	landslide	scrapbook	downpour	chainsaw
greenhouse	eyebrow	pineapple	outfit	seagull	dragonfly

1 Which **list** words contain smaller words that mean…?

a cutting tool ______________ a seeing organ ____________

a mythical beast ______________ not in ______________ ______________

to slip ______________ the ocean ______________ ______________

2 These **list compound words** are mixed up. Can you unscramble them?

cardbrow	overapple	____________________	____________________
everygreen	chainground	____________________	____________________
sealight	spothorse	____________________	____________________
fairsaw	everybody	____________________	____________________
pineboard	eyehead	____________________	____________________

3 Which **list** words are **antonyms** (opposite) for…?

underneath __________________________ nobody __________________________

deciduous __________________________ shadows __________________________

4 Which **list** words mean…?

an amusement park ____________________ thick, stiff paper ____________________

heavy rain ____________________ avalanche ____________________

a fish ____________________ a tropical fruit ____________________

a book for clippings, cards etc. ____________________ an insect ____________________

Word Building

1 Add ***every*** to the following words to form new words.

______________ body ______________ where

______________ one ______________ day

2 Add ***sea*** to the following words to form new words.

___________ horse ______________ gull

___________ breeze ____________ farer

___________ weed ___________ serpent

___________ sick ____________ shore

Strategy

Make word sums.
For example:
fair + ground = fairground.

Challenge

flameproof
bubblegum
livestock

And the gnat, and the dragonfly too,
With all their relations, green, orange and blue.
(William Roscoe)

1 Use **list** and **challenge** words to complete this Wordcross.

Down

1 amusement park

Across

1 not easily burnt
2 avalanche
3 warm place to grow plants
4 heavy rain
5 set of clothes
6 having leaves all year long
7 an insect

2 Unjumble these **list** words.

b o o k s c r a p ____________ a p p l e p i n e ____________

s a w c h a i n ____________ b o a r d c a r d ____________

g u l l s e a ____________ l i g h t s p o t ____________

3 Can you identify the **list** words from these pictures?

____________ ____________ ____________

4 Write an interesting sentence containing any three **list** words.

____

Word Knowledge

1 How many words can you write to describe bubblegum? For example: sticky.

____

2 Make a list of the livestock you might find on a farm.

____

General Knowledge

Use reference materials (encyclopaedias, dictionaries, the Internet etc.) to help you list five of each of the following—the first is done for you.

Insects	Fish	Seabirds	Fruits	Evergreen Trees
dragonfly	seahorse	seagull	pineapple	fir

Prefixes: un and re

Your List

unhappy	undo	unfair	unfold	uneven	unless
repeat	rewind	reverse	retreat	reduce	reflect

1 The **prefix *un*** means not, or opposite. Which **list** words mean…?

to take apart ______________ not fair ______________

not even ______________ not happy ______________

2 The **prefix *re*** means once more, or back. Which **list** words mean…?

make lower or fewer ______________ to throw back light ______________

to do again ______________ to withdraw ______________

to wind back ______________ to go backwards ______________

3 Write in alphabetical order: ***repeat***, ***reflect***, ***rewind*** and ***reduce***.

____

4 Write **antonyms** (opposites) for these words:

advance ______________ absorb ______________ increase ______________

5 Write an interesting sentence containing any three **list** words.

____

Word Building

Add ***ly*** to the following words to make new words.
Then write your new word in a sentence.

unfair + ly ______________

____

uneven + ly ______________

____

unhappy (i) + ly ______________

____

unfortunate + ly ______________

____

Strategy

Split the word into **prefix** and the rest of the word.
For example: unfair = un + fair.

Challenge

unfortunate unnecessary revise revive

History repeats itself.
(Proverb)

1 Which **list** words would fit in these Wordframes?

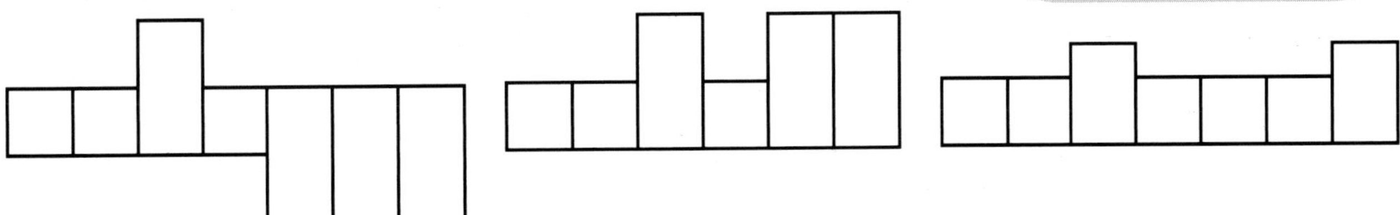

2 Find all the **list** and **challenge** words beginning with the **prefix *re*** in this Wordsearch.

R	R	E	V	I	V	E	R	E	T	R	E	P	E	A	T	R	E	D	U
R	E	R	E	T	R	E	A	T	R	E	W	I	N	R	E	D	U	C	E
R	R	E	V	E	R	S	E	R	E	V	R	E	W	I	N	D	R	E	F
R	E	W	I	N	R	E	F	L	E	C	T	R	R	E	V	I	S	E	R

3 Choose a suitable **list** word to write in the gaps in these sentences.

Some of the younger children were unable to ______________ their wet shoelaces.

When the camera operator realised that the lions had noticed him, he thought it best to ______________ to a safer position.

It was difficult to roll the ball along the ______________ surface.

After the tape had finished, I was asked to ______________ it and listen to it once more.

4 Complete these **list** words.

__ __ __ eat   __ __ fair   __ __ flect   __ __ wind   __ __ do

Word Knowledge

Which **list** or **challenge** words are **base words** for the following?

reflection ______________   revision ______________

reduction ______________   repetition ______________

General Knowledge

1 Which colour reflects light best, black or white? ______________

2 What does the symbol ◀◀ usually represent in technology? ______________

3 Why is it important to reduce carbon emissions? ______________

____

Classroom Unit 36 Contractions

Your List

you'll	they'll	we'll	I'll	he'll	she'll
we're	you're	they're			
I'd	she'd	he'd	we'd	they'd	

Strategy

Think about which letters the **apostrophe** might be replacing.

1 Match the following with **list** words.

they are ________ you are ________ we are ________ I had ________

they had ________ we had ________ she had ________ he had ________

I will ________ you will ________ she will ________ he will ________

we will ________ they will ________

2 Write a suitable **list** word to fill in the gaps in these sentences.

If Mary doesn't hurry ________ be late for work.

Nicky was late for the bus because ________ slept in.

' ________ get your morning newspaper immediately Sir,' said the newsagent.

Although sharks are fascinating creatures, ________ also very dangerous.

Mum, Dad and I climbed through the window because ________ left our key inside.

3 Re-write the following **list** words correctly.

yo'ure ________ the'yll ________ shel'l ________

were ________ youl'l ________ theyre ________

4 Write the following **list** word in your own sentences.

he'll ________

they'd ________

I'd ________

Word Building

Write the **list** words, in the following groups, in full. The first one is done for you.

Those people:	they had	they will	they are
Us:	w ________	w ________	w ________
The male:	h ________	h ________	
The female:	s ________	s ________	
That person:	y ________	y ________	y ________
Me:	I ________	I ________	

Challenge

weren't

> Go abroad and you'll hear news of home.
> (Proverb)

1 Re-write these sentences. Change the underlined words to **contractions**.

Helen would have fallen from the cliff face if she had not had a firm grip.

____

They will have to stop their dog chasing the cat.

____

We had brought out gifts to give to Peter before the party started.

____

2 Write the following **contractions** in full.

he'll __________ they're __________ I'd __________

we're __________ you'll __________ they'd __________

3 Draw a line from the **list** word to its meaning.

I'll	they will
we'd	were not
he'd	I will
they'll	you have
weren't	we would or we had
you've	he had or he would

Word Knowledge

1 Write one sentence containing: ***weren't***.

____

2 Which letters have been replaced by the **apostrophe** in the following **contractions**?

he'll ________ they're ________ they'll ________

I'd ________ *or* ________

she'd ________ *or* ________

weren't ________ you'll ________

General Knowledge

Which nursery rhyme or fairytale character would have said the following?

1 'Oh dear, I'll cry if I don't find my sheep.' ____________________

2 'Oh my! What great big teeth you've got!' ____________________

3 'Who's been eating my porridge and gobbled it all up?' ____________________

4 Classroom Review

Your List

loan	pick	relax	unload	slapping	everywhere	they've
lone	calf	remind	untie	dragging	footpath	they're
waist	kind	subtract		dropping	something	couldn't
waste	grate	superpower	undercover		homework	
herd						
heard						

1 Write the **list** words that would come between ***loan*** and ***slapping*** in a dictionary.

loan ______________________________ ***slapping***

2 Write the six **list** words that are **compound words**.

____

3 Add the **suffix *ing*** to the following words.

slap ____________ drag ____________ drop ____________

4 Write one sentence which shows the meaning of both ***heard*** and ***herd***.

____

5 Which **list** words mean…?

lower back part of leg ____________ young cow ____________

a digging tool ____________ choose ____________

6 Write in full:

couldn't ____________ they've ____________ they're ____________

7 Circle the correct word in this sentence.

The sailor had received a bank (loan/lone) to help finance his (loan/lone) trip around the world.

8 Write one sentence containing any two **list** words.

____

Word Building

Add the endings shown in brackets to the following words.

subtract (ion) ____________ knot (ing) ____________

remind (er) ____________ comfort (able) ____________

kind (ness) ____________

zigzag (ing) ____________

lone (ly) ____________

suburb (an) ____________

Challenge

broadcast suburb rebound
knotting zigzagging
uncanny uncomfortable

Home Study Review

Waste not want not.
(Proverb)

Classroom Review 4

1 Which **list** words are shown here?

______ ______ ______ ______

2 Which **list** words mean…?

to take a load off ______ to make remember ______

school work done at home ______ undo a knot ______

by oneself ______ walkway ______

give something expecting it to be returned ______

3 Write the following **list** words in sentences.

grate (metal frame) ______

grate (rub into small pieces) ______

waste ______

waist ______

Word Knowledge

Which **list** or **challenge** words would best fit into these groups?

television, radio, P.A. ______ strange, weird, unusual ______

reef, granny, hitch, bowline ______

Paddington, Rosehill, Norwood, Fitzroy, Footscray ______

General Knowledge

1 Which two nations were regarded as superpowers during the 'Cold War'?

______

2 Cross out the *incorrect* answer.

If you subtract an even number from an even number, the result will be an (even/odd) number.

If you subtract an odd number from an odd number, the result will be an (even/odd) number.

If you subtract an even number from an odd number, the result will be an (even/odd) number.

Spelling Reference List

A
addresses
adult
advance
aerodrome
affair
afternoon
agree
agreed
air
airport
alleys
alone
aloud
amaze
anxiety
ape
appeal
appoint
approach
aren't
ark
arrange
arrow
ask
astound
atlases
avoid
aware

B
babies
background
badge
balance
bald
bare
barge
bark
barricade
bask
basketball
baulk
bawl
beam
bedtime
beginning
behave
bellow
below
belt
bench
berries
beware
biceps
bicycle
bilingual
bird
birthdays
blackout
blade
blare
blaze
bleach
bleak
bleat
bleed
blew
blouse
blow
blue
boast
boil
bolt
bone
bookshelves
born
borrow
bough
bought
boundaries
bow
bowl
brake
branch
branches
bread
breadth
break
breath
breed
brew
bridge
briefcase
brisk
broadcast
brought
brushes
bubblegum
build
bulb
bump
bunches
buoys
burn
burrow
bushes
busk

C
calf
calm
calves
camp
can't
cane
cape
card
cardboard
care
casket
caught
cell
centuries
ceremonies
chainsaw
chair
champ
chance
change
charge
chart
check
cheque
cherries
chest
chew
child
children
chime
choice
chopping
chrome
churches
circuses
clamp
clashes
clasp
classes
clench
cloak
clockwork
cloud
clown
coach
coast
cockroach
cocoa
coil
coin
cold
companies
compare
conceal
cone
console
cope
cork
corn
could
could've
couldn't
countries
cowl
crane
crate
crawl
cream
creche
creek
creep
crew
cried
crime
crises
crisp
croak
cross
crouch
crown
crunch
crusade
cupboard
curfew
curlew
currant
current
cyclone

D
dairies
dairy
daisies
dance
dare
dark
dart
daylight
daze
dead
deal
debate
debonair
decade
declare
decoys
decree
degree
delays
desk
dew
diaries
didn't
die
difficult
discreet
disk
displays
distance
distraught
disturb
dodge
doesn't
dole
dome
don't
donkeys
downpour
downstairs
dragging
dragonfly
draught
dread
dreadful
drench
dresses

drew
dropping
drought
dump
dusk
dwarf

E
earthenware
edge
elevate
elf
elves
encroach
engulf
ensnare
entrance
escape
esteem
evergreen
everybody
everything
everywhere
ewe
exchange
extraordinary
eyebrow

F
factories
fair
fairground
fairly
fairy
families
fare
farm
feat
feather
feet
fellow
felt
fern
ferries
few
file
firm
flair
flameproof
flapping
flashes
flask
fleet
flew
flies
flinch
float
flounder
flour
flow
foil
fold
follow
footpath
forge
fort
fortnight
fortresses
forward
fought
fowl
foxes
fraught
freak
freedom
fried
fringe
furrow

G
galleys
gasp
gaze
geese
gentlemen
glance
glare
gloat
glow
gnome
gold
golf
gorge
gown
grape
grasp
grate
grave
graze
greed
greenhouse
greet
grew
grime
gripping
groan
grow
growl
grown
guarantee
guard
guesses
gulf
gulp

H
hadn't
hair
half
halt
halves
hard
hare
harm
harp
hatches
hawk
he'd
he'll
head
headlight
headline
heal
heard
heart
heat
hedge
help
herb
herd
herself
hide
highway
himself
hinge
hisses
hobbies
hoedown
hoist
hold
hole
holidays
hollow
home
homework
hope
hope
horn
hour
howl
hulk
humane
hunch
hurricane
hurt

I
I'd
I'll
ideal
inch
inflate
insane
instead
invade
invoice
isn't
itself

J
jamboree
jewel
jewellery
jockeys
join
joist
journey
judge
jump
juries

K
kaleidoscope
kind
kiosk
knee
knew
knight
knives
knotting
know
knowledge
known

L
lair
lamp
landslide
lane
large
lawn
lead (as in need)
leaf
league
leak
lean
leap
leash
least
leather

leaves
ledge
lemonade
leprechaun
libraries
lice
lie
lifeboat
lifetime
lighthouse
lime
limelight
limp
lisp
lives (as in dives)
livestock
loaf
loan
loathe
loaves
lone
lope
lord
lump
lunch

M

magpie
mane
mare
mark
marshes
mask
match
matches
maze
meadow
meal
meantime
measure
melt
memories
men
messes
meter
metre
mice
microphone
microscope
mildew
milk
millionaire
mime
mind
mistake
mistime
moist
mole
monkeys
mope
mould
munch
musk
myself
mysteries

N

narrow
naughty
neat
need
nephew
new
newspaper
night
nightmare
nineteen
noise
nought

O

oath
obelisk
oil
ointment
once
operate
orange
ought
our
ourselves
outfit
overhead
overnight
overtime
owl
own
oxen

P

pair
palm
pantomime
park
part
pastime
peace
peach
peak
periscope
pew
phone
pick
pie
piebald
piece
pied
piety
pillow
pinch
pineapple
plane
planning
plate
platypuses
playtime
pleasant
pleasure
plotting
plough
plunge
poach
point
poise
poison
pole
port
post
pouch
pouches
pound
prairie
prepare
prime
prince
proceed
prodding
pronoun
pronounce
proud
prowl
pullover
pump
punch

Q

queen
quench
questionnaire
quoit

R

radishes
rainforest
ranch
range
rare
rasp
ready
real
rear
rebound
recoil
redeem
reduce
reflect
refugee
rejoice
relax
relays
remind
renew
renown
repair
repeat
replies
retreat
return
reveal
reverse
revise
revive
reward
rewind
ridge
right
risk
rissole
roast
role
rope
row
running

S

salt
sandwiches
scapegoat
scare
scarf
science
scope
scoundrel
scout
scrap
scrapbook
scrape
scratch
scrawl
screech

screen
screw
scroll
scrub
scruffy
scrumptious
seagull
seahorse
seal
seam
seas
seize
sell
selves
shape
share
shark
sharp
shave
shawl
she'd
she'll
sheaves
sheep
shelf
shelves
shirt
shoal
shoplift
shopping
short
should
should've
shouldn't
shout
shown
shred
shrew
shrewd
shrill
shrivel
shroud
shrub
shrug
silk
silkworm
since
sinew
skate
skewer
skipping
skirt
slapping
slave
sleep
slime
slipping
slope
snapping
snow
soak
society
soil
sold
something
sometime
sorrow
sort
sought
sow
spade
spanning
spare
spark
sparring
sparrow
speech
speed
spell
spinning
splashes
splitting
spoil
sponge
sport
spotlight
spout
sprawl
spray
sprays
spread
spring
sprint
sprout
square
squeal
squirm
squirt
stagecoach
stairs
stamp
staple
stare
starring
state
steadfast
steady
steal
steep
stench
stepping
stethoscope
stew
stick
stirring
stomp
stone
stopping
stories
storm
stout
stow
strange
strap
straw
strawberries
stray
streak
stream
street
strict
string
strip
stroll
strong
struck
strum
stump
sublime
submarine
submerge
subscription
subtitle
subtract
suburb
subway
subzero
superb
superficial
supermarket
supernatural
superpower
supersonic
superstar
superstition
surf
surge
swamp
swapping
sweep
sweet
swimming
sword
syndrome

T

talk
tape
task
taught
taxes
teepee
teeth
telephone
telescope
that's
their
themselves
there
they'd
they'll
they're
they've
thieves
thoroughfare
thought
thousand
thrash
thread
threadbare
threat
three
threw
thrill
thrive
throat
throb
throbbing
throne
throttle
through
throughout
throw
thrown
thrust
thump
tie
tilt
time
to
toast
toil
toilet
tomorrow
tone
tongue-tied
too
torches
tosses
touches

tow
towards
town
trade
train
tramp
trawl
tread
treasure
treat
trench
tried
trophies
trotting
trousers
trout
trudge
turf
turkeys
turn
tusk
tweed
two

U

uncanny
uncomfortable
underarm
undercarriage
undercover
underground
undergrowth
underline
underwear
undo
uneven
unfair
unfold
unfortunate
unhappy
uniform
unless
unload
unnecessary
untie
upstairs
urge

V

valleys
varnishes
vault
vibrate
voice
void
volt

W

waist
wallow
warm
warn
warp
wasp
waste
watches
we'd
we'll
we're
weapon
wear
weather
weatherboard
welfare
weren't
wheelbarrow
whelp
where
where's
which
whipping
who's
whole
wild
will-o'-the-wisp
winch
wisp
witch
wizard
wives
wolf
wolves
women
won't
wood
word
work
world
worm
worn
worshipping
would
wouldn't
wrench
wretches
write
wrought

X

Y

yawn
yeast
yellow
you'll
you're
you've
yourself
yourselves

Z

zealot
zigzagging
zone

My Personal Word List

Here are some common words you need to learn how to spell.

among whom during although either though your

Student Profile

At this level the student's knowledge of:

...is	Not Apparent	Emerging	Consolidating	Established
'magic **e**' words				
words with dipthongs:				
ee				
ow (**blow**)				
oa				
ai				
ea (**bean**)				
ea (**head**)				
ie (**tie**)				
ew				
words with **ou** (**out**)				
words with **oi** (**oil**)				
initial consonant blends:				
str scr spr shr thr				
final consonant blends:				
sp sk				
rt rd rm rn rk rf rp rb				
lt ld lk lf lb lm lp				
wn wl wk mp				
nch				
dge nge rge nce				
ght				
Plurals: adding **es**				
Plurals: **y** to **i** and add **es**				
Plurals: vowel then **y**				
Plurals: **f/fe** to **ves**				
Plurals: change of spelling				
Homophones				
Homographs				
Prefixes: **super sub under bi un re**				
Suffixes: adding **ing**				
Contractions				
Compound words				
Comments				

Spelling Guide

The English language has grown from many languages so it is difficult to have a set of hard and fast rules for learning to spell.

Rather than being spelling rules, the following is a guide for spelling. Many so-called rules of spelling have exceptions,, so it is best to learn the guide and remember the exceptions.

1 To add ***ing*** to words ending with ***e***, drop the ***e*** then add ***ing***.
For example: skate—skating, dodge—dodging, stare—staring, write—writing

Exceptions:
If there is a vowel before the last ***e***. For example: seeing, canoeing.

2 To add ***ing***, ***ed*** or ***er*** to words ending with a consonant, double the consonant.
For example: stir—stirring; span—spanning; plot—plotting; stop—stopped, stopping; travel—traveller, travelling, travelled; run—runner, running.

Exceptions:
- **a** Words ending with a vowel then ***w***. For example: rowed, screwed, chewing, flowing, growing.
- **b** Words ending with a vowel then ***x***. For example: boxer, boxed, boxing, taxed, fixing.
- **c** Words ending with a vowel then ***y***. For example: saying, annoyed, prayer.
- **d** When there are TWO vowels before the last consonant, do not double the last letter. For example: repairing, screening, sleeping, squealed, threaded, treated.

3 Put ***i*** before ***e*** when the sound is ***e*** and they do not follow ***c***.
For example: piece, field, believe, achieve.

Exceptions:
seize
Put ***e*** before ***i*** after ***c***.
For example: receive, ceiling, deceive.

Exceptions:
eight, either, neither, height, weight, freight, weird, rein, their

4 *Plurals*
- **a** Words ending in ***s ss sh ch x z***, add ***es***.
- **b** Words ending in ***y*** following a consonant, change the ***y*** to ***i*** then add ***es***.
- **c** Words ending in ***y*** following a vowel, add ***s***.
- **d** Words ending in ***f*** or ***fe***, change ***f*** or ***fe*** to ***v*** then add ***es***.

Exceptions:
chiefs, dwarfs, roofs, gulfs, staffs
- **e** Some words have a change of basic spelling.
- **f** Words ending in ***o*** add ***es***. For example: heroes, potatoes, tomatoes.

Exceptions:
Words from languages other than English. For example: pianos, kimonos.

Glossary

acrostic	a sentence or poem, in which the first letters of the words, or line, spell a word
adjectives	words that describe name words (nouns) (for example: *tiny* room, *dark* eyes, *magnificent* sunset)
adverb	words used to tell us more about action and feeling words (verbs) (for example: ran *quickly*, jump *now*, felt *lonely*)
antonym	a word having the opposite meaning to another
apostrophe	(i) a sign showing a letter (or letters) have been left out (') (ii) a sign showing that something is owned (for example: Terry's book)
base word	the word from which others may come (for example: *circle*—circular)
challenge	a group of words that belong to the same family as the list words, but may be more challenging to master
compound word	a word made up of two words (for example: foot + ball = football)
consonant	letters of the alphabet that are not vowels
consonant blend	two or more letters that are not vowels (*a e i o u*) that make one sound (for example: drum, scream, inspect)
contraction	shortened form of words in which an apostrophe represents missing letters
homograph	a word that is spelt the same as another word but has a different meaning (for example: bear—carry, bear—animal)
homonym	a word that has the same sound or spelling as another word but a different meaning (for example: right, write)
homophone	two words that sound the same (for example: right, write)
list words	a group of words with a similarity in spelling
nouns	words that name something (for example: chair, book, country, house)
onomatopoeia	a word written the same as it sounds (for example: phew)
palindrome	a palindromic word is one that is spelt that same backwards and forwards (for example: noon, madam)
past tense	words that say what has happened
plural	a word that means more than one (for example: bunches, boys, foxes)
prefix	a word part which, when placed in front of a word, changes its meaning (for example: *dis* + interest = disinterest)
prime	of the first importance
suffix	a word part which, when added to the end of a word, changes it meaning (for example: sad + *ness* = sadness)
syllable	part of a word that contains a vowel sound or a consonant acting as a vowel (for example: along = a/long)
synonym	a word having a similar meaning to another
verb	a word that tells you about an action (for example: walk, hear)
vowel	the letters *a e i o u*

Spelling Matters—Book 4 (3rd Edition) Answers

Unit	Page	Answers
1	6	**1** blaze, daze, gaze, graze, maze **2** lane/a narrow road, crane/a bird or a machine for lifting, cape/a cloak, escape/get away, ape/an animal, grape/ a fruit, invade/enter or attack as an enemy, cane/a thin wooden stick **3** behave, escape **4** grate, great, main, mane, plain, plane **WB** trading, scraping, blazing, grazing, shaving, escaping
1	7	**1** Teacher **2** cape, grape, maze **3** Teacher **WK** decade, vibrate, insane, lemonade, elevate, debate **GK 1** They are all states. **2** Dane **3** Cape York, Cape Horn, Cape of Good Hope
2	8	**1** hare, pair, hair, mare, mayor, wear **2** scare, share, spare, square, stare **3** Teacher **WB** farewell, scarecrow, awareness, careful, careless, nightmare
2	9	**1** blare, share, spare, scare, rare, glare, stare, care **2** daring, caring, baring, sharing, sparing, staring, glaring, blaring, preparing **3** blare, spare, glare **WK** earthenware, ensnare, thoroughfare, threadbare, nightmare **GK 1** Ireland **2** hare **3** Sydney
3	10	**1** chime, grime/prime/crime, slime **2** Teacher **3** bedtime, meantime, lime, prime, chime, mime **4** grimy, slimy (Teacher) **WB** overtime, lifetime, timekeeper, playtime, timetable
3	11	**1** Teacher **2** chime, slime, crime **WK** Teacher; answers will vary (first school, first or main minister, first or earliest development) **GK 1** dime **2** time **3** pantomime
4	12	**1** Teacher **2** dome, dole, scope, alone **3** rissole, chrome, aerodrome, alone, mope, throne, zone **4** cope, lope, mope, scope **WB** coping/coped sloping/sloped phoning/phoned loping/loped zoning/zoned hoping/hoped
4	13	**1** gnome, whole **2** bone, dome, home **3** *Across:* 1 dole 4 mope 5 zone *Down:* 1 dome 2 lope 3 home **WK** syndrome cyclone console **GK** telescope/to look at things far away, microscope/to look at small things, stethoscope/to monitor the heart and lungs, periscope/to look around or about, oscilloscope/to look at to and fro movements, kaleidoscope/to look at beautiful patterns
5	14	**1** greet, creek, breed, creep, nineteen, screech **2** sheep, sleep, speech, speed, sweep **3** Teacher **4** agree/tepee/queen, nineteen/refugee, freedom/proceed street/ screech/screen, guarantee **5** Teacher (tweed/a coarse, woollen cloth, decree/an official order, discreet/tactful, careful in speech and actions, redeem/to get back in payment or get back in favour) **WB** bred, sped, crept, slept, bled, swept
5	15	**1** sweep, sleep, creep, steep greed, need, agreed, speed, proceed, bleed sweet, fleet, street, discreet **2** esteem, sleep, greet, teeth, speed, screech, creek, street, sweep **3** Teacher **WK** tepee, decree, degree, tweed **GK 1** They are all breeds of sheep. **2** It was a speech given by US president Abraham Lincoln during the American Civil War. **3** in the knee

Spelling Matters—Book 4 (3rd Edition) Answers

Unit	Page	Answers
6	16	**1** shout, scoundrel, thousand, bough, pronounce, astound **2** flower, flour **3** stout, trout, spout, scout, sprout, shout, throughout **4** thousand, throughout, trousers, trout **5** stout, trout, spout, scout, shout, cloud, proud, flour, bough, pouch blouse **WB 1** shrouded **2** Teacher (possible answers: outside, throughout, outhouse, pout, shout, stout, trout, blackout etc.)
6	17	**1** shroud, shout, stout, cloud, drought **2** trousers, flour, plough, stout, flounder, proud **3** pronoun, flounder, astound, scoundrel **4** drought, shout, proud **WK** sprout, shout, scoundrel, trout, pouch **GK 1** scout **2** eat **3** over
7	18	**1** sow, yellow, tow, own, row, bow, sparrow, throw, narrow **2** Teacher **3** arrow, borrow, follow, hollow, pillow **WB** sowing/sower/sowed, slowing/slower/slowed, bowling/bowler/bowled
7	19	**1** Teacher **2** arrow, sparrow, grow, narrow, borrow, sorrow, wheelbarrow, tomorrow, furrow, burrow **3** grow, tomorrow, below, snow/tow, sow, arrow/bow **WK** Teacher **GK 1** shot put, javelin, hammer (basketball, handball—possibly other ball sports such as tennis, volleyball etc.) **2** yesterday **3** Port Philip Bay
8	20	**1** croak, cloak, coast, toast, approach, cocoa **2** Teacher **3** roast, throat, boast, loathe **4** oath, float, coast, boast **WB** coastal, boastful, afloat, approachable
8	21	**1** *Across:* 3 croak 4 toast 5 oath *Down:* 1 boast 2 float 3 coast **2** poach **3** encroach, shoal, loathe, cockroach, gloat **4** Teacher **WK 1** floatation (can also be spelt flotation), approachable **GK 1** throat **2** Teacher **3** Teacher
9	22	**1** repair, fair **2** pair, repair, lair, air **3** Teacher **4** chair, fair, fairly, fairy, lair **5** lair, fairy, pair, dairy **6** downstairs/upstairs **WB** airport, airway, aircraft, airlift, airtight, airship, air conditioner, armchair, chairlift, downstairs, fairway, fairground, fairytale, uplift, upstairs (Port Fairy)
9	23	**1** air/the gases we breathe, heir/one who inherits, hair/threadlike growth from the skin, hare/rabbit-like animal, pair/two of a kind, pare/to peel, pear/a fruit, flair/natural talent or smart style, flare/suddenly burn brightly, stairs/steps, stares/to look at directly **2** Teacher **WK** debonair, affair, prairie, fairly **GK 1** Tinkerbell **2** oxygen/nitrogen (accept carbon dioxide) **3** *The Little House on the Prairie*
10	24	**1** Teacher **2** seem, seam, peak, peek, feat, feet **3** peach, seal, bleat, peak, cream, leash **WB** mislead, misdeal, mistreatment ideally, really, neatly unleash, unreal
10	25	**1** Teacher **2** sea, ash, pea, veal, tea, east **3** squeal, bleach, streak **WK** Teacher **GK 1** yeast **2** Australian Football League, National Rugby League, Returned Servicemen's League **3** Sir Edmund Hillary, Neil Armstrong
11	26	**1** thread, leather, head, meadow **2** bread, dread, ready, spread, thread, tread **3** weather, tread, instead, ready **4** unsteady, alive, unpleasant **5** Yes, Yes (probably), No **WB** headache, headquarters, headstrong, headphones, headline, headland, forehead, headway Teacher

Spelling Matters—Book 4 (3rd Edition) Answers

Unit	Page	Answers
11	27	**1** bread, thread, feather **2** tape measure, treasure chest, breathtaking **3** tread, pleasure/breath, treasure/meadow **WK** readily, steadily, dreadfully, steadfastly **GK 1** thread **2** steady **3** leather
12	28	**1** hoist, choice, moist, poise, soil, point, toil, quoit **2** toilet, voice, poison, avoid **3** poison, toilet **4** coin, oil, join **WB 1** boiled/boiling, toiled/toiled, oiled/oiling, foiled/foiling, coiled/coiling, joined/joining **2** unavoidable, moisture, noiseless, pointless, appointment
12	29	**1** *Across:* 1 oil 2 poison 5 toilet 7 void 9 coil 10 toil 11 boil *Down:* 1 ointment 3 soil 4 noise 6 invoice 8 foil **2** join, moist, toil **3** appoint, point, poise, poison **WK** rejoice, foil, joist, invoice **GK 1** It's a poison obtained from a herb. **2** quoits **3** broiling **WH** potion
13	30	**1** Teacher **2** fried, science, piety, magpie **3** lie, tie, anxiety, pied, society, science **4** tries, cries, fries **5** piebald, flies **WB** spies, cries, butterflies, sties, skies, flies, dragonflies, tries
13	31	**1** flies, tie, lie, magpie, pie, pied, anxiety **2** Teacher (a respect and honour for religion) **3** Teacher **WK** society, anxiety, piety **GK 1** Pied Piper **2** astronomy **3** Magpie Lark
14	32	**1** screw (crew), jewel (ewe) **2** nephew, flew, ewe, crew, chew **3** ewe, threw, nephew **4** Teacher **WB 1** few/fewer/fewest, blow/blew/blown, new/newer/newest, know/knew/known, throw/threw/thrown, grow/grew/grown
14	33	**1** screw, ewe, jewel **2** jewel **3** crew, new, stew **4** blew, grew, brew, knew, chew, stew, crew, screw, drew, threw, flew, shrewd, skewer, shrew, ewe **5** shrew, curlew, curfew **WK** grandfather, aunt (aunty), nephew, brother, sister-in-law **GK 1** Jew **2** phew **3** trews
R1	34	**1** chair, chew, cloak, crate, crime **2** Teacher **3** crime, stout, sweet, least, noise **4** know, fried, role **5** Teacher
R1	35	**1** thousand, steep, scrape **2** thousand, crate, chair, cloak, least, slave **3** fried, crate, least, measure **4** crime, alone, crate, know, least, role **5** jamboree, scapegoat **WK** scare, scrape **GK 1** pyrotechnics (fireworks) **2** temperature/thermometer; time/watch, clock, sundial; mass/scales **3** Any of the ruminants (cattle, deer, sheep etc.)
15	36	**1** throne, scruffy, stroll, sprint, shred, thrust **2** scrap, shrug, spray, sting, strip **3** three, through, stroll, thread, throne **4** throb, shred, straw, shrug, strip, thrash, stray **WB 1** strawberry, scrapbook, awesome, hairspray, heartthrob **2** throbbing, scrapping, strumming, shredding, strapping, stripping, scrubbing, shrugging
15	37	**1** Teacher **2** spray, shrub, spring **3** stroll, scruffy, shrill, three, thrill, scroll, throttle string, spring **4** spring, throne, throb, straw **WK** throttle, thrive, strict, shrivel, scroll **GK 1** thrice **2** Thrace **3** strum (musical instrument)

Spelling Matters—Book 4 (3rd Edition) Answers

Unit	Page	Answers
16	38	**1** wasp, flask brisk, crisp ask, desk risk, bask **2** grasp, mask, wisp, rasp, task, lisp **3** No, No, Yes **WB 1** gasped/gasping, clasped/clasping, lisped/lisping, basked/basking, risked/risking, grasped/grasping, asked/asking, rasped/rasping **2** Teacher
16	39	**1** brisk, flask, lisp **2** obelisk, casket **3** Teacher **4** desk, busk **WK** wispy, crispy, risky crispy carrots, risky rescue, wispy clouds **GK 1** asp **2** rasp **3** They are all types of wasp.
17	40	**1** cork, herb, bird, heart, shark, return **2** farm, chart, born **3** skirt, shirt, scarf **4** worm, work, warm **5** forward, dark, sharp, hard **6** harp, port **WB** cardboard, hardboard, swordfish, hardwood, farmhouse, turnstile, fortnight, shorthand, heartache
17	41	**1** Teacher **2** sort, part, turn, short, burn, mark **3** farm, harm, warm **WK 1** cardboard, discard, placard, cardiac, cardigan **2** squirm, warp, sword, superb **GK 1** An ark **2** Ord River **3** a uniform
18	42	**1** elf, bulb, volt, golf, gulp, gulf **2** sort, half, palm, talk **3** Teacher **4** fold, halt, world, bald **5** palm, calf, milk, cold **WB 1** should not, could not, would not **2** elves, calves, halves, wolves
18	43	**1** *Across:* 1 gold 4 felt 5 wolf 6 build 7 bald *Down:* 2 difficult 3 elf 4 crease 6 bulb **2** belt, world, milk, palm **3** True, False, False **WK 1** Teacher **2** Teacher **GK 1** Gulf War (Second) **2** a wolf **3** vixen
19	44	**1** lawn, clamp, scrawl, limp **2** fowl, howl, own, gown, hawk/owl **3** scrawl, shown, sprawl, stamp, stump, swamp **4** clamp, stamp, crown, owl, stump **5** True, False, True **WB** shown, thrown, blown, sown, mown, flown, grown, known
19	45	**1** Teacher **2** Teacher **WK** Answers may vary—slapstick clown, bejewelled crown/gown, sleepy yawn/town/clown/owl etc., sharp-eyed hawk, bright lamp, mown lawn **GK 1** rubbing a lamp **2** pawns **3** on a dance floor
20	46	**1** bench, branch, clench, crunch, hunch **2** Teacher **3** pinch, clench, lunch, punch, stench **4** Teacher **5** stench, branch, pinch **WB** winches, benches, branches, ranches, lunches, punches, trenches, pinches, hunches
20	47	**1** Teacher **2** flinch, crunch, stench **3** winch, hunch, inch, drench **WK** Teacher **GK** Anthropology/humankind, Biology/living organisms, Astronomy/heavenly bodies, Geology/earth, Archaeology/civilisation through material remains, Sociology/society, Ornithology/birds, Zoology/animals
21	48	**1** bridge, ledge, gorge, barge, strange, prince **2** Once, judge, fringe **3** dance, judge, ridge, orange, gorge, prince **4** Answers will vary (narrow river valley with steep sides/to eat greedily) **WB** charging, glancing, plunging, dodging, dancing, barging, advancing, exchanging, balancing
21	49	**1** once, gorge, judge, bridge **2** bridge, plunge, glance **WK** advance, entrance, sponge, trudge, urge, exchange, balance, knowledge, distance, orange **GK 1** lodge **2** Sydney, London, San Francisco **3** Geikie/WA, Katherine/NT, Jasper/NT, Wittenoom/WA

Spelling Matters—Book 4 (3rd Edition) Answers

Unit	Page	Answers
22	50	**1** draught, bought, brought, taught, caught **2** False **3** brought, caught, taught, bought **WB** bought, brought, thought, fought, caught, taught (Teacher)
22	51	**1** fortnight, thought **2** fought, taught, fortnight, sought, ought, draught, nought **3** Teacher **4** naughty, draught, fortnight **WK** fraught, wrought, distraught **GK** Answers may vary. WW1—Britain, Australia, USA, France, New Zealand, Canada; WW2—Britain, Australia, USA, Canada, New Zealand; Gulf War 2003—USA, Britain, Australia, Denmark and others
R2	52	**1** Teacher **2** tilt, child, firm, turf, fern, dusk, vault, forge **3** scratch, shelf, spark, squirt, strong **4** sprint = print, in grasp = rasp, as, asp known = know, now, no, own spark = spa, spar, park, ark **5** strong, throat, thump, tilt, turf **6** throat, vault, firm **WB** scratched, sprinted, known, brought, thumped, squirted, tilted, forged, vaulted
R2	53	**1** Teacher **2** Teacher **3** brought, sport, forge **WK 1** wand, musk **2** a driving or forceful inward flow of the sea **GK 1** Teacher **2** French **3** Dorothy
23	54	**1** Teacher **2** atlases, hisses, tosses, watches, churches **3** splashes, circuses, flashes/clashes, pouches **WB** branched/branches/branching, clashed/clashes/clashing, guessed/guesses/guessing, tossed/tosses/tossing, matched/matches/matching
23	55	**1** atlases, brushes, bushes, clashes, taxes, watches **2** splashes, watches, brushes **3** hatches, churches, watches, circuses, radishes, branches **4** Teacher **WK 1** fortresses, addresses **2** platypuses, fortresses, sandwiches, radishes **GK 1** peaches **2** ostriches **3** witches
24	56	**1** Teacher **2** ferries, hobbies, countries, daisies, diaries, factories **3** diaries, centuries, countries, juries **WB 1** raspberries, blackberries, blueberries, gooseberries, boysenberries, cranberries **2** hobbies, libraries, companies, countries, ceremonies, memories, daisies, trophies
24	57	**1** daisies, factories, trophies, strawberries **2** dairies, daisies, diaries **3** *Across:* 1 dairies 4 ferries 7 libraries 8 diaries *Down:* 1 daisies 2 trophies 3 factories 4 families 5 strawberries 6 hobbies **WK** juries, trophies, hobbies, ferries, daisies **GK 1** wallabies **2** nurseries **3** dictionaries
25	58	**1** Teacher **2** alleys, donkeys, sprays, turkeys, valleys **3** Teacher **4** relays, holidays, monkeys **5** birthdays, highways, sprays, delays **WB** highways, seasprays (seaways), alleyways, birthdays
25	59	**1** alleys, monkeys, turkeys, valleys, journeys, donkeys, galleys; sprays, holidays, delays, relays, birthdays, highways; buoys **2** alleys, delays, birthdays **3** Teacher **WK 1** Teacher **2** highways, galleys, buoys, journeys **GK 1** drays **2** subways **3** Teacher
26	60	**1** Teacher **2** shelves, thieves, calves, wolves, loaves, elves, halves **3** Teacher **4** lives, loaves, shelves, wives, wolves **WB** yourselves, themselves, ourselves
26	61	**1** Teacher **2** Teacher **WK** gulfs, dwarfs, staffs, chiefs (Teacher: hooves/hoofs, wharves/wharfs) **GK 1** sheaves **2** six **3** wolves

Spelling Matters—Book 4 (3rd Edition) Answers

Unit	Page	Answers
27	62	**1** foot/feet, mouse/mice, woman/women, goose/geese, man/men, tooth/teeth, ox/oxen, child/children, louse/lice **2** mice, oxen, children, lice **3** lice, teeth, mice, geese, oxen **4** Teacher **WB** oxen, children, women, geese, feet, men
27	63	**1** children, feet, men, mice, oxen, teeth **2** women, geese, teeth **3** mice, geese, oxen **4** crisis—a time of trouble or worry or a turning point in something **WK** geese, oxen, feet, teeth **GK 1** an insect/6, a spider/8, a bird/2, a snake/0 **2** lice **3** teeth
R3	64	**1** Teacher **2** The children used their torches to find their way. It is dangerous to leave sharp knives near babies. The displays showed bunches of cherries. **3** Teacher **4** marshes, jockeys, replies, stories, displays, knives **WB** strawberry/strawberries, bookshelf/bookshelves, fairy story/fairy stories, field mouse/field mice, carving knife/carving knives
R3	65	**1** Teacher (missing word = knives) **2** marshes **3** mice, cherries, displays, children, thieves, berries **4** Teacher **WK** mysteries, decoys, boundaries, bookshelves, wretches, varnishes **GK 1** jockeys **2** fairy stories/fairy tales **3** They are all mice.
28	66	**1** threw/through/through, write/right, their/there/their, our/hour, wood/would, which/witch/witch, brake/break, piece/peace, where/wear **2** knight, night, metre, meter **WB** peaceful, kilometre, breakfast, firewood, knighthood, rightful, nightfall, centimetre, meterbox, whereabouts, overseas, seizure
28	67	**1** Teacher **2** right/write/night/knight, which/witch, threw/through/blue/blew/to/too/two **3** Teacher **4** Teacher **5** Teacher **WK** currant, brake, metre/hour, blue, meter, cell, seize **GK 1** metre, metre, metre **2** They are all seas. **3** a knight
29	68	**1** basketball, clockwork, overnight, everything, cupboard, silkworm, lighthouse, afternoon, stagecoach, headlight **2** Teacher **3** clockwork, pullover, lifeboat, afternoon, everything, rainforest, headlight, daylight **4** background, lighthouse, overnight **WB 1** cupboard, springboard, surfboard, chalkboard, overboard **2** daylight, headlight, lighthouse, lightweight, lightyear
29	69	**1** rainforest, pullover, clockwork **2** lifeboat, stagecoach, background, afternoon **3** afternoon, airport, background, basketball, briefcase, briefcase **WK** rainforest, briefcase, pullover, basketball, extraordinary, airport, tongue-tied **GK 1** airport, clockwork **2** basketball **3** Queensland
30	70	**1** supermarket, supersonic, supernatural, superstar **2** underground, underline, undergrowth, underwear, underarm **3** subway, subtitle, submarine, submerge, subzero **4** Teacher (the definition should contain the word 'two') **5** two **6** Teacher **WB** underdeveloped, undercarriage, underclothes, underhand, undertow, underworld, underwater, underpass
30	71	**1** underline, superstar, underarm **2** underwear, supermarket, bicycle, underarm, submarine **3** underground, underwear, supermarket, superstar **WK** underground, subway, supernatural, submarine **GK 1** arm **2** bicycles **3** yes

Spelling Matters—Book 4 (3rd Edition) Answers

Unit	Page	Answers
31	72	**1** Teacher **2** prodding, stepping, gripping, stopping, whipping, planning/plotting, swapping, beginning, spinning **3** swimming, plotting/planning, flapping, chopping/splitting **WB** whipped, skipped, flapped/flapping, stepped/stepping, gripped/gripping, throbbed/throbbing, snapped/snapping
31	73	**1** flapping, splitting/throbbing, spinning, snapping **2** planning plotting prodding **3** Teacher **4** Teacher **5** shopping, slipping, whipping, planning, skipping, chopping, stepping, stirring **WK** starring, spanning, worshipping, sparring **GK** **1** swimming **2** running **3** trotting
32	74	**1** where's, shouldn't, you've, who's, don't, wouldn't, that's, they've, can't, isn't, didn't, hadn't, doesn't, won't **2** Teacher **3** Teacher **WB** couldn't, Don't, That's, can't
32	75	**1** Teacher **2** where is, they have, did not, can not, should not, do not, that is, is not, will not **3** didn't, doesn't, don't, they've, that's **4** shouldn't, they've **WK** Teacher **GK** Teacher
33	76	**1** hide, spell, cross, punch, match, rear, chest, post, cape, file, seal, loaf, mind, mole, train, stick **2** spell, mind, match, cross **WB** **1** filing, hiding, stapling **2** matches, loaves, crosses, punches **3** postcard, spellbound, tea chest, matchstick, meatloaf
33	77	**1** file, post, punch, chest **2** Teacher **WK** seal, punch, cape, train, vault **GK** **1** pole vault, gymnastics (vaulting horse), possibly accept steeplechase **2** vault/safe **3** pound **4** pound
34	78	**1** chainsaw, eyebrow, dragonfly, blackout/outfit, landslide, seahorse/seagull **2** cardboard, overhead, everybody, chainsaw, seahorse, spotlight, fairground, evergreen, pineapple, eyebrow **3** overhead, everybody, evergreen, spotlight **4** fairground, cardboard, downpour, landslide, seahorse, pineapple, scrapbook, dragonfly **WB** **1** everybody, everywhere, everyone, everyday **2** seahorse, seagull, seabreeze, seafarer, seaweed, seaserpent, seasick, seashore
34	79	**1** *Down:* 1 fairground *Across:* 1 flameproof 2 landslide 3 greenhouse 4 downpour 5 outfit 6 evergreen 7 dragonfly **2** scrapbook, pineapple, chainsaw, cardboard, seagull, spotlight **3** spotlight, fairground, seahorse **4** Teacher **WK** **1** Teacher **2** Teacher **GK** Teacher
35	80	**1** undo, unfair, uneven, unhappy **2** reduce, reflect, repeat, retreat, rewind, reverse **3** reduce, reflect, repeat, rewind **4** retreat, reflect, reduce **5** Teacher **WB** unfairly, unevenly, unhappily, unfortunately (Teacher)
35	81	**1** unhappy, unfold, retreat **2** Teacher **3** undo, retreat, uneven, rewind **4** repeat, unfair, reflect, rewind, undo **WK** reflect, revise, reduce, repeat **GK** **1** white **2** rewind **3** to reduce greenhouse gases which are believed to be causing climate change
36	82	**1** they're, you're, we're, I'd, they'd, we'd, she'd, he'd, I'll, you'll, she'll, he'll, we'll, they'll **2** she'll, he'd/she'd, I'll, they're, we'd **3** you're, they'll, she'll, we're, you'll, they're **4** Teacher **WB** we'd/we'll/we're, he'd/he'll, she'd/she'll, you'd/you'll/you're, I'd/I'll

Spelling Matters—Book 4 (3rd Edition) Answers

Unit	Page	Answers
36	83	**1** she'd, They'll, We'd **2** he will/shall, they are, I had/I would, we are, you will/you shall, they had/they would **3** I'll/I will, we'd/we would *or* we had, he'd/he had *or* he would, they'll/they will, weren't/were not, you've/you have **WK 1** Teacher **2** wi/sha, a, wi/sha, woul/ha, woul/ha, o, wi/sha **GK 1** Bo Peep **2** Wolf **3** one of the three bears (baby)
R4	84	**1** lone, pick, relax, remind **2** superpower, undercover, everywhere, footpath, something, homework **3** slapping, dragging, dropping **4** Teacher **5** calf, calf, pick, pick **6** could not, they have, they are **7** loan, lone **8** Teacher **WB** subtraction, knotting, reminder, comfortable, kindness, zigzagging, lonely, suburban
R4	85	**1** footpath, pick, subtract, calf **2** unload, remind, homework, untie, lone, footpath, loan **3** Teacher **WK** broadcast, uncanny, untie, suburb **GK 1** USA and Soviet Union **2** even, even, odd